AMIGURUMI
CHRISTMAS ORNAMENTS

AMIGURUMI
CHRISTMAS ORNAMENTS

40 Crochet Patterns for Keepsake Ornaments
with a Delightful Nativity Set, North Pole Characters,
Sweet Treats, Animal Friends and Baby's First Christmas

LINDA WRIGHT

Dedicated to Mom and Dad in memory of our Merry Christmases

Also by Linda Wright
Toilet Paper Origami
Toilet Paper Origami On a Roll
Amigurumi Golf Club Covers
Amigurumi Toilet Paper Covers
Amigurumi Animal Hats
Amigurumi Animal Hats Growing Up
Honey Pie Amigurumi Dress Up Doll with Picnic Play Set
Honey Bunny Amigurumi Dress Up Doll with Garden Play Mat

Credits
Photography: Randy and Linda Wright

All rights reserved. Permission is granted to copy or reprint portions for any noncommercial use, except they may not be posted online without permission. You may sell the finished products that you make yourself at your local bazaar, craft fair, etc. but not on the internet. Items cannot be mass produced without the publisher's written permission. Contact the publisher with licensing inquiries.

Copyright © 2020 Linda Wright
Edition 2.0

Lindaloo Enterprises
P.O. Box 90135
Santa Barbara, California 93190
United States
sales@lindaloo.com

ISBN: 978-1-937564-15-5
Library of Congress Control Number: 2020912063

CONTENTS

Introduction	6
General Directions	7
Supplies	8
Abbreviations	9
Gauge	9
How to Read a Pattern	9

Nativity Set

Star of Bethlehem	12
Angel	14
Shepherd	15
Baby Jesus	17
Mary	18
Joseph	19
Wiseman I	20
Wiseman II	21
Wiseman III	22
Ox	23
Donkey	25
Sheep	26

North Pole Characters

Santa Claus	30
Mrs. Claus	31
Reindeer	32
Elf	34
Snowman	35
Gingerbread Man	36
Toy Soldier	37

Sweet Treats

Candy Cane	42
Mistletoe Truffle	43
Snow Cone	44
Snowflake Macaron	45
Ribbon Candy	46
Starlight Peppermint	47
Taffy Twirl	48
Pinwheel Pop	49
Cut-Out Cookies	50

Animal Friends

Snowy Owl	58
Mouse	59
Lion	60
Snowshoe Hare	61
Fox	62
Camel	64
Polar Bear	66
Cat	67
Dog	68
Penguin	69

Baby's First Christmas

Baby Girl	72
Baby Boy	74

Stitches	76
Techniques	79
Resources	81
Yarn	81

INTRODUCTION

Christmas ornaments add fun and festivity to the holiday season—the more, the merrier! And when they're handmade, they become more meaningful. Amigurumi Christmas Ornaments make great gifts—and precious keepsakes that you, your family and your friends can cherish.

You'll find 40 patterns in this collection for delightful baubles that capture the spirit of the season. There's a 12-piece Nativity Set; Santa Claus and other familiar faces from the North Pole; colorful cookies and candies; and adorable animals. For Baby's First Christmas, I've included ornaments to personalize with any color of hair and a tag with the baby's name and date of birth.

Amigurumi Christmas Ornaments range in size from 3" to 5" when made with the materials described. If you'd like to change their size, you can do so by using a smaller or larger crochet hook—or a different yarn weight. Just be sure to use a crochet hook that matches your yarn.

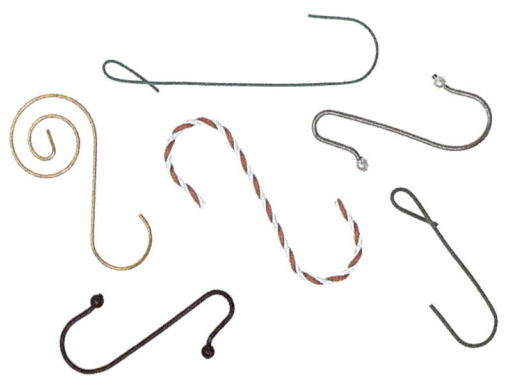

For hanging, these ornaments are finished with a small metal ring. The ring will easily attach to your favorite style of wire ornament hanger, or a loop of ribbon, metallic cord or twine.

The patterns for my Sweet Treats were written with a featured color scheme, but these are at their best when made in lots of different combinations. Even Candy Canes come in more colors than the traditional red and white!

This book has been a twinkle in my eye for a long time and I'm excited to bring it to fruition. Like all of my books, it was a labor of love. I sincerely hope these projects fill your hearts and hands with hours of happy crocheting. I also hope they decorate your Christmas trees for many years to come.

If you enjoy these patterns, please let me know by leaving a review at your online place of purchase. Other customers would appreciate it too!

Now, gather up your yarn and let's get started!

GENERAL DIRECTIONS

Before starting your first ornament, be sure to read through the next 2 introductory pages plus the Stitches and Techniques sections at the back of the book. You will find many helpful tips.

If you're new to crocheting and like to learn by watching, YouTube.com offers a treasure trove of excellent crocheting tutorials. These are also great for experienced crocheters who need to brush up. I have assembled a collection of my favorite videos on Pinterest. You can view them at www.pinterest.com/LindalooEnt/ on a board named Amigurumi Tutorials. I've also pinned some of my favorite supplies there.

Amigurumi is meant to be crocheted rather tightly. This prevents polyester fiberfill from showing thru the stitches of stuffed pieces. When you stuff an ornament, pack it very full. Fiberfill compresses in time and you'll want your ornaments to stay shapely. After fastening off, add even more fiberfill thru the tiny hole that remains. A pair of long tweezers is my favorite tool for this (see page 8). Add as much stuffing as you can—it's amazing how much will fit! Then, when you think you're done, *try to add more*!

For the first time, I'm using the Invisible Decrease (invdec) in some of my patterns. This decrease is a more discreet way to eliminate a stitch than my typical sc2tog. You can, however, interchange the methods and use whichever you prefer. Instructions for both decreases are provided in the Stitches section at the back of the book.

It is standard procedure in amigurumi to leave long tails of yarn when you fasten off. These yarn tails, or even sewing thread, can be used when it comes time to sew the pieces of a project together. Invisible sewing thread made of transparent nylon or polyester is especially nice when sewing pieces of different colors together.

This book uses U.S. crochet terms. If an instruction says sc, that is a U.S. single crochet—or a U.K. double crochet. Please refer to the stitch diagrams at the back of the book to be sure you are making the stitches as intended.

SUPPLIES

Yarn

These projects take such little bits of yarn that you will likely be using yarns that you have on hand. Most of the patterns call for Worsted-weight yarn (#4), but several times a lighter weight is used. Please check each pattern for the yarn weight specification(s). For your reference, the yarns that I used are provided at the back of the book. I especially loved the colors, texture, loft and sheen of Lion Brand "Vanna's Choice" yarn for these ornaments.

Crochet Hook

The following hooks are used: F5/3.75mm and G6/4mm. My favorite hook is the **Clover Soft Touch**. I love the thick handle and the shape of the head which inserts easily into a stitch.

Yarn Needle

You will need a large-eyed needle to sew the various pieces of your items together and also to finish them off by weaving the loose ends into your work. Yarn needles with a blunt point are readily available but I frequently like to use one with a sharp point. These can be hard to find in stores, so if you'd like one, plan to shop online. My favorite is the Size 14 Chenille or Embroidery needle.

Stitch Markers

Stitch markers are used to keep track of where a round or row of crochet begins and ends. You can use a bobby pin, safety pin or purchased stitch markers. Making the correct number of stitches is important, so count to double check if ever you're not sure.

Safety Eyes & Noses

Plastic safety eyes & noses give amigurumi a professional look. Each comes with a post section and a washer, but for these projects, I prefer attaching them with glue. You can leave the post intact for gluing—or cut it off with wire cutters. Apply glue to fabric, set eye or nose in position & apply pressure. Black animal eyes can be substituted for triangle animal noses if desired.

Glue

Glue is used for some of the assembly. Choose a clear-drying craft glue. **Fast Grab Tacky Glue** is great for attaching plastic embellishments such as eyes, acrylic jewels and beads. **Fabri-Tac** is wonderful for joining fabric to fabric. **Hot glue** is a good all-purpose choice. With any glue, I recommend practicing with scraps before working on your actual project to become familiar with how the glue reacts. If using hot glue, you will want to know how to prevent the formation of messy strings. Video demos of various methods are available on YouTube. Tip: release trigger of glue gun and move tip in small rapid circles to break string before pulling gun away from your work.

Sewing Box Basics

You will need a small pair of sharp scissors, straight pins, a ruler, sewing needle and thread.

Row Counter

Well worth the investment, a row counter keeps track of what round or row of the pattern you are crocheting. A pencil and paper can also be used. Crochet apps for mobile devices are available too. A simple Android app that I like is called Minimalist Stitch Counter.

Removable Notes

Use small sticky notes to keep track of your place in a pattern. Every time you complete a round or a row, move the note down to reveal the next line of instructions. I wouldn't work without one!

Stuffing & Stuffing Tools

Polyester fiberfill is used for stuffing these ornaments. It is soft, plush and very light weight. This makes it ideal for items that will hang on the branch of a tree. The eraser end of a new pencil, a blunt-tipped chopstick or tweezers make great stuffing tools. I highly recommend a pair of 6-inch straight-tip serrated tweezers. I find them invaluable for inserting stuffing thru small openings.

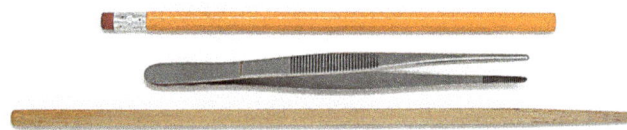

ABBREVIATIONS

The following abbreviations are used:

1st = first
2nd = second
w/ = with
yd = yard
st = stitch
ch = chain
sc = single crochet
hdc = half double crochet
dc = double crochet
tr = triple or treble crochet
lp st = loop stitch
sl st = slip stitch
rnd = round
invdec = invisible decrease
sc2tog = single crochet 2 stitches together
sc3tog = single crochet 3 stitches together
hdc2tog = half double crochet 2 stitches together
dc2tog = double crochet 2 stitches together
sp = space
yo = yarn over
* * = a set of stitches
( ) = stitch count; also indicates a group of sts worked together in the same stitch or space

GAUGE

Exact gauge is not essential for these projects.

HOW TO READ A PATTERN

Each round or row is written on a new line. Most rounds have a repeated section of instructions that are written between two asterisks *like this*. The instruction between the asterisks is to be repeated as many times as indicated before you move on to the next step. At the end of a round, the total number of stitches to be made in that round is indicated in parentheses (like this).

Let's look at a round from a pattern.

Rnd 6: *sc in next 4 sts, 2 sc in next st* 6 times (36 sts).

This means:

Rnd 6	This is the 6th round of the pattern.
sc in next 4 sts	Make 1 single crochet stitch in each of the next 4 stitches
2 sc in next st	Make 2 single crochet stitches, both in the same stitch
6 times	Repeat everything between * and * 6 times.
(36 sts)	The round will have a total of 36 stitches.

So, following the instructions for Round 6, you will:

single crochet in the next 4 sts, 2 sc in the next st,
single crochet in the next 4 sts, 2 sc in the next st,
single crochet in the next 4 sts, 2 sc in the next st,
single crochet in the next 4 sts, 2 sc in the next st,
single crochet in the next 4 sts, 2 sc in the next st,
single crochet in the next 4 sts, 2 sc in the next st,

for a total of 36 stitches.

Nativity Set

Star of Bethlehem

The lovely plump star begins with the creation of 5 small cones. These are connected to form the points. Next, the front and back of the star are filled in by working in rounds.

SUPPLIES

G6/4mm crochet hook

50 yds of Worsted weight yarn in yellow

Polyester fiberfill stuffing

Jump ring, 10mm

POINTS (MAKE 5)

Be sure to keep piece turned right-side out as you go.

Make a magic ring, ch 1.

Rnd 1: 4 sc in ring, pull ring closed tight (4 sts).

Rnd 2: *sc in next st, 2 sc in next st* twice. Place marker for beginning of rnd and move marker up as each rnd is completed (6 sts).

Rnd 3: *sc in next 2 sts, 2 sc in next st* twice (8 sts).

Rnd 4: *sc in next 3 sts, 2 sc in next st* twice (10 sts).

Rnd 5: *sc in next 4 sts, 2 sc in next st* twice (12 sts).

Rnd 6: *sc in next 5 sts, 2 sc in next st* twice (14 sts).

Rnd 7: *sc in next 6 sts, 2 sc in next st* twice (16 sts).

Rnd 8: sc in each st around.

Sl st in next st. Fasten off with long tail. Tuck tails inside.

MARKING THE POINTS

When the Star is assembled, 4 sts on each Point are left unworked. By marking the sts to be skipped, it's easy to identify them.

Cut 10 pieces of contrasting yarn to use as markers.

On each Point, locate the final sl st. Counting clockwise from the sl st, hook a marker thru Sts 7-8 and Sts 15-16 (see Fig. A).

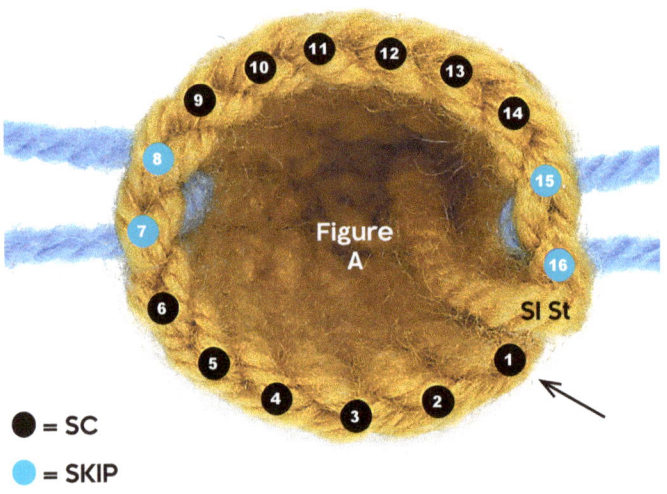

● = SC
● = SKIP

STAR FRONT

To connect Points for Star Front, work in Sts 1-6 of each Point (see Fig. A).

Rnd 1: take any Point, join with sc in first st (see arrow, Fig. A), sc in next 5 sts. Repeat with remaining Points (30 sts).

The assembly will now look like Fig. B.

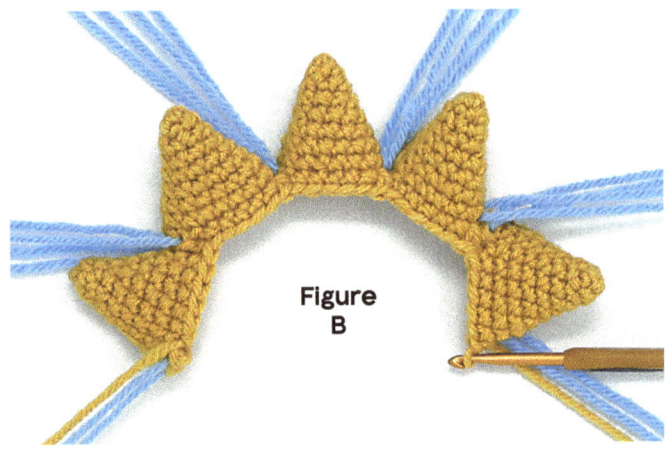

Start Rnd 2 in first st of next Point (see Fig. C).

Figure C

Rnd 2: *sc in next 4 sts, invdec* 5 times. Place marker for beginning of rnd and move marker up as each rnd is completed (25 sts).

Rnd 3: *sc in next 3 sts, invdec* 5 times (20 sts).

Rnd 4: *sc in next 2 sts, invdec* 5 times (15 sts).

Rnd 5: *sc in next st, invdec* 5 times (10 sts).

Sl st in next st. Fasten off.

Figure D

To close hole (see Fig. D), thread tail in yarn needle, insert needle thru front loop of each st around opening & pull tight. Secure with a knot on wrong side. Trim excess tail.

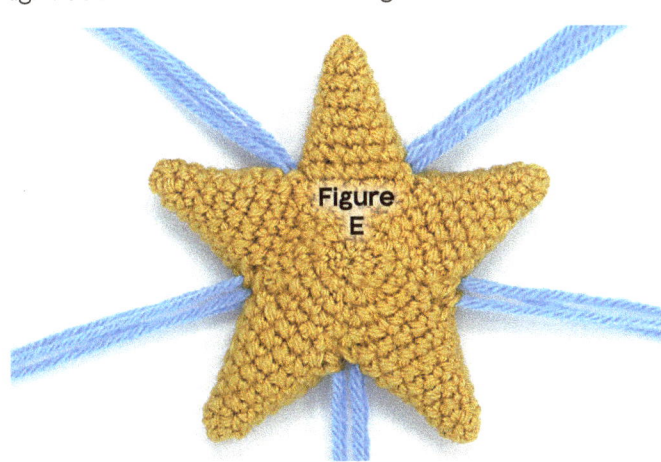

Figure E

The Star Front is done (see Fig. E).

STAR BACK

To connect the Points for Star Back, work in Sts 9-14 (see Fig. A) of each Point.

As you work Rnd 1, be sure to skip over the sts that are marked with contrasting yarn.

Rnd 1: starting with any Point, join with sc in first st (see arrow, Fig. F), sc in each st around. Place marker for beginning of rnd and move marker up as each rnd is completed (30 sts).

Figure F

Rnd 2: *sc in next 4 sts, invdec* 5 times (25 sts).

Pause to close holes between Points: Remove marker-yarn. Pull out long tails tucked inside Points, use them to sew holes closed and secure each with a knot. Trim excess from tails.

Rnd 3: *sc in next 3 sts, invdec* 5 times (20 sts).

Rnd 4: *sc in next 2 sts, invdec* 5 times (15 sts).

Stuff the Star.

Rnd 5: *sc in next st, invdec* 5 times (10 sts).

Sl st in next st. Fasten off. Finish adding stuffing.

To close hole, thread tail in yarn needle, insert needle thru front loop of each st around opening & pull tight. Secure tail inside Star.

FINISHING

Squeeze Star into shape.

Attach jump ring (see page 80).

ANGEL

SUPPLIES

G6/4mm crochet hook

Worsted weight yarn in beige and yellow

2 black safety eyes, 8mm

2" brass craft ring

Glue (see page 8)

Invisible sewing thread

Polyester fiberfill stuffing

Jump ring, 10mm

HEAD

With yellow yarn, make a magic ring, ch 1.

Rnd 1: 6 sc in ring, pull ring closed tight (6 sts).

Rnd 2: 2 sc in each st around. Place marker for beginning of rnd and move marker up as each rnd is completed (12 sts).

Rnd 3: *sc in next st, 2 sc in next st* 6 times (18 sts).

Rnd 4: *sc in next 2 sts, 2 sc in next st* 6 times (24 sts).

Rnd 5: *sc in next 3 sts, 2 sc in next st* 6 times (30 sts).

Rnd 6: *sc in next 4 sts, 2 sc in next st* 6 times (36 sts).

Rnds 7-9: sc in each st around; change to beige yarn in last st.

Rnds 10-13: sc in each st around.

Rnd 14: *sc in next 4 sts, invdec* 6 times (30 sts).

Rnd 15: *sc in next 3 sts, invdec* 6 times (24 sts).

Start to stuff and continue stuffing after each rnd.

Rnd 16: *sc in next 2 sts, invdec* 6 times (18 sts).

Rnd 17: *sc in next st, invdec* 6 times (12 sts).

Rnd 18: invdec 6 times (6 sts).

Fasten off. Finish adding stuffing.

To close hole, thread tail in yarn needle, insert needle thru front loop of each st around opening and pull tight. Weave in end.

Squeeze Head into a nice round shape.

BUN

With yellow yarn, make a magic ring, ch 1.

Rnd 1: 6 sc in ring, pull ring closed tight (6 sts).

Rnd 2: 2 sc in each st around. Place marker for beginning of rnd and move marker up as each rnd is completed (12 sts).

Rnd 3: *sc in next st, 2 sc in next st* 6 times (18 sts).

Rnds 4-6: sc in each st around.

Rnd 7: *sc in next st, invdec* 6 times (12 sts).

Fasten off. Stuff the Bun.

FINISHING

Glue on eyes between Rnds 11-12 with an interspace of 7-8 sts.

With beige yarn, embroider nose 2 rows below eyes.

Sew Bun to top of Head.

Place brass craft ring on Head encircling Bun. Sew in place with invisible thread by making 1 st over each quadrant of ring.

Attach jump ring (see page 80).

SHEPHERD

SUPPLIES

G6/4mm crochet hook

Worsted weight yarn in beige, taupe, green and red

2 black safety eyes, 8mm

Glue (see page 8)

Polyester fiberfill stuffing

Coffee mug and teaspoons

Jump ring, 10mm

Note: A ch 1 at the beginning of a row is for turning your work and does not count as a st.

HEAD

With taupe yarn, make a magic ring, ch 1.

Rnd 1: 6 sc in ring, pull ring closed tight (6 sts).

Rnd 2: *sc in next st, 2 sc in next st* 3 times. Place marker for beginning of rnd and move marker up as each rnd is completed (9 sts).

Rnd 3: *sc in next 2 sts, 2 sc in next st* 3 times (12 sts).

Rnd 4: *sc in next 2 sts, 2 sc in next st* 4 times (16 sts).

Rnd 5: *sc in next 3 sts, 2 sc in next st* 4 times (20 sts).

Rnd 6: *sc in next 4 sts, 2 sc in next st* 4 times (24 sts).

Rnd 7: *sc in next 5 sts, 2 sc in next st* 4 times (28 sts).

Rnd 8: *sc in next 6 sts, 2 sc in next st* 4 times (32 sts).

Rnd 9: *sc in next 7 sts, 2 sc in next st* 4 times; change to beige yarn in last st (36 sts).

Rnds 10-15: sc in each st around; change to taupe yarn in last st.

Rnds 16-19: sc in each st around.

Start to stuff and continue stuffing after each rnd.

Rnd 20: *sc in next 4 sts, invdec* 6 times (30 sts).

Rnd 21: *sc in next 3 sts, invdec* 6 times (24 sts).

Rnd 22: *sc in next 2 sts, invdec* 6 times (18 sts).

Rnd 23: *sc in next st, invdec* 6 times (12 sts).

Rnd 24: invdec 6 times (6 sts).

Fasten off. Finish adding stuffing.

To close hole, thread tail in yarn needle, insert needle thru front loop of each st around opening and pull tight. Weave in end. Squeeze Head into shape.

HEAD CLOTH

With green yarn, make a magic ring, ch 1.

Rnd 1: 6 sc in ring, pull ring closed tight (6 sts).

Rnd 2: 2 sc in each st around. Place marker for beginning of rnd and move marker up as each rnd is completed (12 sts).

Rnd 3: *sc in next st, 2 sc in next st* 6 times (18 sts).

Rnd 4: *sc in next 2 sts, 2 sc in next st* 6 times (24 sts).

Rnd 5: *sc in next 3 sts, 2 sc in next st* 6 times (30 sts).

Rnd 6: *sc in next 4 sts, 2 sc in next st* 6 times (36 sts).

Rnd 7: *sc in next 5 sts, 2 sc in next st* 6 times (42 sts).

Rnds 8-11: sc in each st around.

Now work in rows.

Rows 12-24: ch 1, turn, sc in next 24 sts (24 sts).

Fasten off.

Edge Trim: with right side up, join at corner opposite where you fastened off Row 24, sc in each st around front edge of Head Cloth. Fasten off. Weave in ends.

TWISTED CORD

A mug is used for a weight when making the Twisted Cord. Fill mug with spoons to make it heavier.

Cut two 30" pieces of yarn: one red and one green. Tie strands together near one end with an overhand knot. Pull spliced strand thru mug handle until knot rests at inside of handle. Tie strands together again with an overhand knot at outside of handle—so that knot is about 2" from handle (see Step 1 photo on next page).

Grasp a yarn tail in each hand several inches from knot.

1. Roll strands between thumb and index finger so that both strands rotate to the **RIGHT**.

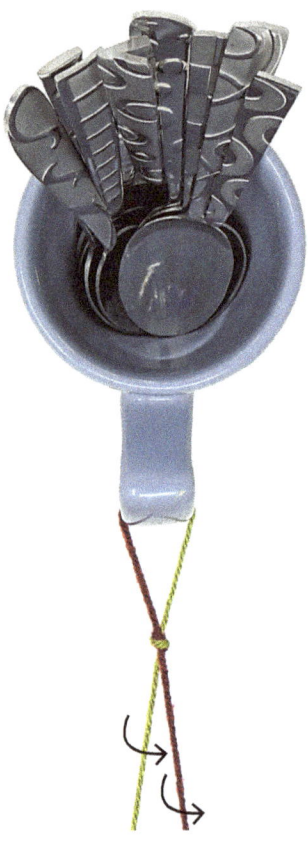

2. When yarn is tightly twisted, wrap **RIGHT STRAND OVER LEFT STRAND** several times until all twisted yarn is wrapped.

Move hands down yarn in 2" increments and repeat Steps 1-2 until you have 16" of twisted cord. Tie strands together with an overhand knot. Trim tails to 1". Cut cord off of mug handle leaving 1" tails.

FINISHING

Sew or glue Head Cloth to Head.

Glue Twisted Cord to Head Cloth as shown in picture and tie ends in a knot at center back.

Glue on eyes between Rnds 13-14 with an interspace of 7-8 sts.

With beige yarn, embroider nose 2 rows below eyes.

Attach jump ring (see page 80).

Baby Jesus

SUPPLIES

G6/4mm crochet hook

Worsted weight yarn in beige and white

2 black safety eyes, 8mm

Glue (see page 8)

Polyester fiberfill stuffing

Jump ring, 10mm

HEAD

With beige yarn, make a magic ring, ch 1.

Rnd 1: 6 sc in ring, pull ring closed tight (6 sts).

Rnd 2: 2 sc in each st around. Place marker for beginning of rnd and move marker up as each rnd is completed (12 sts).

Rnd 3: *sc in next st, 2 sc in next st* 6 times (18 sts).

Rnd 4: *sc in next 2 sts, 2 sc in next st* 6 times (24 sts).

Rnd 5: *sc in next 3 sts, 2 sc in next st* 6 times (30 sts).

Rnd 6: *sc in next 4 sts, 2 sc in next st* 6 times (36 sts).

Rnds 7-13: sc in each st around.

Rnd 14: *sc in next 4 sts, invdec* 6 times (30 sts).

Rnd 15: *sc in next 3 sts, invdec* 6 times (24 sts).

Start to stuff and continue stuffing after each rnd.

Rnd 16: *sc in next 2 sts, invdec* 6 times (18 sts).

Rnd 17: *sc in next st, invdec* 6 times (12 sts).

Rnd 18: invdec 6 times (6 sts).

Fasten off. Finish adding stuffing.

To close hole, thread tail in yarn needle, insert needle thru front loop of each st around opening and pull tight. Weave in end.

Squeeze Head into a nice round shape.

HEAD WRAP

With white yarn, make a magic ring, ch 1.

Rnd 1: 6 sc in ring, pull ring closed tight (6 sts).

Rnd 2: 2 sc in each st around. Place marker for beginning of rnd and move marker up as each rnd is completed (12 sts).

Rnd 3: *sc in next st, 2 sc in next st* 6 times (18 sts).

Rnd 4: *sc in next 2 sts, 2 sc in next st* 6 times (24 sts).

Rnd 5: *sc in next 3 sts, 2 sc in next st* 6 times (30 sts).

Rnd 6: *sc in next 4 sts, 2 sc in next st* 6 times (36 sts).

Rnd 7: *sc in next 5 sts, 2 sc in next st* 6 times (42 sts).

Rnds 8-14: sc in each st around.

Fasten off. Weave in end.

FINISHING

Glue on eyes between Rnds 10-11 with an interspace of 7-8 sts.

With beige yarn, embroider nose 2 rows below eyes.

Cover final rnds of Head with Head Wrap; sew or glue in place at an angle as pictured.

Attach jump ring (see page 80).

Mary

SUPPLIES

G6/4mm crochet hook

Worsted weight yarn in beige, brown and pink

2 black safety eyes, 8mm

Glue (see page 8)

Polyester fiberfill stuffing

Jump ring, 10mm

HEAD

With brown yarn, make a magic ring, ch 1.

Rnd 1: 6 sc in ring, pull ring closed tight (6 sts).

Rnd 2: 2 sc in each st around. Place marker for beginning of rnd and move marker up as each rnd is completed (12 sts).

Rnd 3: *sc in next st, 2 sc in next st* 6 times (18 sts).

Rnd 4: *sc in next 2 sts, 2 sc in next st* 6 times (24 sts).

Rnd 5: *sc in next 3 sts, 2 sc in next st* 6 times (30 sts).

Rnd 6: *sc in next 4 sts, 2 sc in next st* 6 times (36 sts).

Rnds 7-9: sc in each st around; change to beige yarn in last st.

Rnds 10-13: sc in each st around.

Rnd 14: *sc in next 4 sts, invdec* 6 times (30 sts).

Rnd 15: *sc in next 3 sts, invdec* 6 times (24 sts).

Start to stuff and continue stuffing after each rnd.

Rnd 16: *sc in next 2 sts, invdec* 6 times (18 sts).

Rnd 17: *sc in next st, invdec* 6 times (12 sts).

Rnd 18: invdec 6 times (6 sts).

Fasten off. Finish adding stuffing.

To close hole, thread tail in yarn needle, insert needle thru front loop of each st around opening and pull tight. Weave in end.

Squeeze Head into a nice round shape.

HEAD SCARF

With pink yarn, make a magic ring, ch 1.

Rnd 1: 6 sc in ring, pull ring closed tight (6 sts).

Rnd 2: 2 sc in each st around. Place marker for beginning of rnd and move marker up as each rnd is completed (12 sts).

Rnd 3: *sc in next st, 2 sc in next st* 6 times (18 sts).

Rnd 4: *sc in next 2 sts, 2 sc in next st* 6 times (24 sts).

Rnd 5: *sc in next 3 sts, 2 sc in next st* 6 times (30 sts).

Rnd 6: *sc in next 4 sts, 2 sc in next st* 6 times (36 sts).

Rnd 7: *sc in next 5 sts, 2 sc in next st* 6 times (42 sts).

Rnds 8-15: sc in each st around.

Fasten off. Weave in end.

FINISHING

Glue on eyes between Rnds 11-12 with an interspace of 7-8 sts.

With beige yarn, embroider nose 2 rows below eyes.

Sew or glue Head Scarf in place as pictured.

Attach jump ring (see page 80).

JOSEPH

SUPPLIES

G6/4mm crochet hook

Worsted weight yarn in beige, brown, blue and cream

2 black safety eyes, 8mm

Glue (see page 8)

Polyester fiberfill stuffing

Coffee mug and teaspoons

Jump ring, 10mm

Note: A ch 1 at the beginning of a row is for turning your work and does not count as a st.

HEAD

With brown yarn, make a magic ring, ch 1.

Rnd 1: 6 sc in ring, pull ring closed tight (6 sts).

Rnd 2: *sc in next st, 2 sc in next st* 3 times. Place marker for beginning of rnd and move marker up as each rnd is completed (9 sts).

Rnd 3: *sc in next 2 sts, 2 sc in next st* 3 times (12 sts).

Rnd 4: *sc in next 2 sts, 2 sc in next st* 4 times (16 sts).

Rnd 5: *sc in next 3 sts, 2 sc in next st* 4 times (20 sts).

Rnd 6: *sc in next 4 sts, 2 sc in next st* 4 times (24 sts).

Rnd 7: *sc in next 5 sts, 2 sc in next st* 4 times (28 sts).

Rnd 8: *sc in next 6 sts, 2 sc in next st* 4 times (32 sts).

Rnd 9: *sc in next 7 sts, 2 sc in next st* 4 times; change to beige yarn in last st (36 sts).

Rnds 10-15: sc in each st around; change to brown yarn in last st.

Rnds 16-19: sc in each st around.

Start to stuff and continue stuffing after each rnd.

Rnd 20: *sc in next 4 sts, invdec* 6 times (30 sts).

Rnd 21: *sc in next 3 sts, invdec* 6 times (24 sts).

Rnd 22: *sc in next 2 sts, invdec* 6 times (18 sts).

Rnd 23: *sc in next st, invdec* 6 times (12 sts).

Rnd 24: invdec 6 times (6 sts).

Fasten off. Finish adding stuffing.

To close hole, thread tail in yarn needle, insert needle thru front loop of each st around opening and pull tight. Weave in end.

Squeeze Head into shape.

HEAD CLOTH

With blue yarn, make a magic ring, ch 1.

Rnd 1: 6 sc in ring, pull ring closed tight (6 sts).

Rnd 2: 2 sc in each st around. Place marker for beginning of rnd and move marker up as each rnd is completed (12 sts).

Rnd 3: *sc in next st, 2 sc in next st* 6 times (18 sts).

Rnd 4: *sc in next 2 sts, 2 sc in next st* 6 times (24 sts).

Rnd 5: *sc in next 3 sts, 2 sc in next st* 6 times (30 sts).

Rnd 6: *sc in next 4 sts, 2 sc in next st* 6 times (36 sts).

Rnd 7: *sc in next 5 sts, 2 sc in next st* 6 times (42 sts).

Rnds 8-11: sc in each st around.

Now work in rows.

Rows 12-24: ch 1, turn, sc in next 24 sts (24 sts).

Fasten off.

Edge Trim: with right side up, join at corner opposite where you fastened off Row 24, sc in each st around front edge of Head Cloth. Fasten off. Weave in ends.

TWISTED CORD

Cut two 30" pieces of yarn: one brown and one cream. Follow instructions on pages 15-16.

WISE MAN I

Melchior

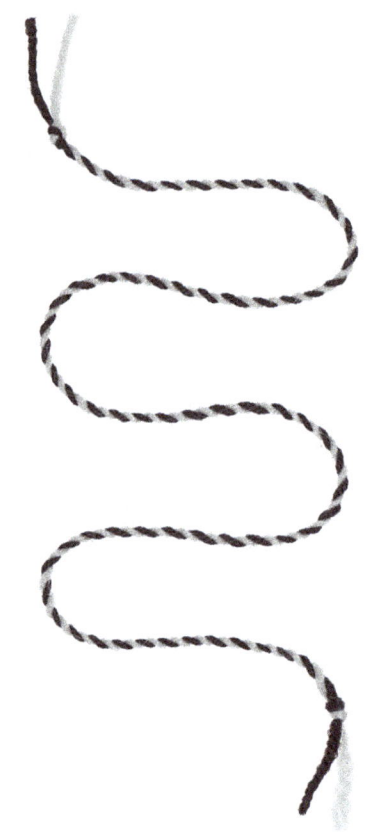

FINISHING

Sew or glue Head Cloth to Head.

Glue Twisted Cord to Head Cloth as shown in pictures and tie ends in a knot at center back.

Glue on eyes between Rnds 13-14 with an interspace of 7-8 sts.

With beige yarn, embroider nose 2 rows below eyes.

Attach jump ring (see page 80).

SUPPLIES

G6/4mm crochet hook

Worsted weight yarn in beige, gray, teal and gold

2 black safety eyes, 8mm

Acrylic craft jewels

Glue (see page 8)

Polyester fiberfill stuffing

Jump ring, 10mm

HEAD

With gray yarn, make a magic ring, ch 1.

Rnd 1: 6 sc in ring, pull ring closed tight (6 sts).

Rnd 2: *sc in next st, 2 sc in next st* 3 times. Place marker for beginning of rnd and move marker up as each rnd is completed (9 sts).

Rnd 3: *sc in next 2 sts, 2 sc in next st* 3 times (12 sts).

Rnd 4: *sc in next 2 sts, 2 sc in next st* 4 times (16 sts).

Rnd 5: *sc in next 3 sts, 2 sc in next st* 4 times (20 sts).

Rnd 6: *sc in next 4 sts, 2 sc in next st* 4 times (24 sts).

Rnd 7: *sc in next 5 sts, 2 sc in next st* 4 times (28 sts).

Rnd 8: *sc in next 6 sts, 2 sc in next st* 4 times (32 sts).

Rnd 9: *sc in next 7 sts, 2 sc in next st* 4 times; change to beige yarn in last st (36 sts).

Rnds 10-15: sc in each st around; change to teal yarn in last st.

Rnds 16-19: sc in each st around.

Start to stuff and continue stuffing after each rnd.

Rnd 20: *sc in next 4 sts, invdec* 6 times (30 sts).

Rnd 21: *sc in next 3 sts, invdec* 6 times (24 sts).

Rnd 22: *sc in next 2 sts, invdec* 6 times (18 sts).

Rnd 23: *sc in next st, invdec* 6 times (12 sts).

Rnd 24: invdec 6 times (6 sts).

Fasten off. Finish adding stuffing.

To close hole, thread tail in yarn needle, insert needle thru front loop of each st around opening and pull tight. Weave in end.

Squeeze Head into shape.

CROWN

★ **SPECIAL STITCH USED IN THIS PATTERN**
SHELL STITCH (3 dc, ch 4, 3 dc)

With gold yarn, ch 42, join with sl st in 1st ch to make a ring using care not to twist the chain.

Rnds 1-2: ch 2, hdc in each st around, join with sl st in top of ch-2 (42 sts).

Rnd 3: ch 3, 2 dc in same st as where your ch started, ch 4, 3 dc in same st as where your initial ch started, skip 2 sts, sc in next st, *skip 2 sts, shell into next st, skip 2 sts, sc in next st* around, join with sl st in top of starting ch-3.

Fasten off. Weave in ends.

FINISHING

Sew Crown to Head as shown in picture. Glue on jewels.

Glue on eyes between Rnds 13-14 with an interspace of 7-8 sts.

With beige yarn, embroider nose 2 rows below eyes.

Attach jump ring (see page 80).

WISE MAN II

Gaspar

SUPPLIES

G6/4mm crochet hook

Worsted weight yarn in tan, charcoal, red and yellow

2 black safety eyes, 8mm

Acrylic craft jewels

Glue (see page 8)

Polyester fiberfill stuffing

Jump ring, 10mm

HEAD

With charcoal yarn, make a magic ring, ch 1.

Rnd 1: 6 sc in ring, pull ring closed tight (6 sts).

Rnd 2: *sc in next st, 2 sc in next st* 3 times. Place marker for beginning of rnd and move marker up as each rnd is completed (9 sts).

Rnd 3: *sc in next 2 sts, 2 sc in next st* 3 times (12 sts).

Rnd 4: *sc in next 2 sts, 2 sc in next st* 4 times (16 sts).

Rnd 5: *sc in next 3 sts, 2 sc in next st* 4 times (20 sts).

Rnd 6: *sc in next 4 sts, 2 sc in next st* 4 times (24 sts).

Rnd 7: *sc in next 5 sts, 2 sc in next st* 4 times (28 sts).

Rnd 8: *sc in next 6 sts, 2 sc in next st* 4 times (32 sts).

Rnd 9: *sc in next 7 sts, 2 sc in next st* 4 times; change to tan yarn in last st (36 sts).

Rnds 10-15: sc in each st around; change to red yarn in last st.

Rnds 16-19: sc in each st around.

Start to stuff and continue stuffing after each rnd.

Rnd 20: *sc in next 4 sts, invdec* 6 times (30 sts).

Rnd 21: *sc in next 3 sts, invdec* 6 times (24 sts).

Rnd 22: *sc in next 2 sts, invdec* 6 times (18 sts).

Rnd 23: *sc in next st, invdec* 6 times (12 sts).

Rnd 24: invdec 6 times (6 sts).

Fasten off. Finish adding stuffing.

To close hole, thread tail in yarn needle, insert needle thru front loop of each st around opening and pull tight. Weave in end.

Squeeze Head into shape.

CROWN

★ SPECIAL STITCH USED IN THIS PATTERN
SHELL STITCH (3 dc, ch 4, 3 dc)

With yellow yarn, ch 42, join with sl st in 1st ch to make a ring using care not to twist the chain.

Rnds 1-2: ch 2, hdc in each st around, join with sl st in top of ch-2 (42 sts).

Rnd 3: ch 3, 2 dc in same st as where your ch started, ch 4, 3 dc in same st as where your initial ch started, skip 2 sts, sc in next st, *skip 2 sts, shell into next st, skip 2 sts, sc in next st* around, join with sl st in top of starting ch-3.

Fasten off. Weave in ends.

FINISHING

Sew Crown to Head as shown in picture. Glue on jewels.

Glue on eyes between Rnds 13-14 with an interspace of 7-8 sts.

With tan yarn, embroider nose 2 rows below eyes.

Attach jump ring (see page 80).

WISE MAN III

Balthazar

SUPPLIES

G6/4mm crochet hook

Worsted weight yarn in brown, black, lavender and purple

2 black safety eyes, 8mm

Acrylic craft jewels

Glue (see page 8)

Polyester fiberfill stuffing

Jump ring, 10mm

HEAD

With black yarn, make a magic ring, ch 1.

Rnd 1: 6 sc in ring, pull ring closed tight (6 sts).

Rnd 2: *sc in next st, 2 sc in next st* 3 times. Place marker for beginning of rnd and move marker up as each rnd is completed (9 sts).

Rnd 3: *sc in next 2 sts, 2 sc in next st* 3 times (12 sts).

Rnd 4: *sc in next 2 sts, 2 sc in next st* 4 times (16 sts).

Rnd 5: *sc in next 3 sts, 2 sc in next st* 4 times (20 sts).

Rnd 6: *sc in next 4 sts, 2 sc in next st* 4 times (24 sts).

Rnd 7: *sc in next 5 sts, 2 sc in next st* 4 times (28 sts).

Rnd 8: *sc in next 6 sts, 2 sc in next st* 4 times (32 sts).

Rnd 9: *sc in next 7 sts, 2 sc in next st* 4 times; change to brown yarn in last st (36 sts).

Rnds 10-15: sc in each st around; change to lavender yarn in last st.

Rnds 16-19: sc in each st around.

Start to stuff and continue stuffing after each rnd.

Rnd 20: *sc in next 4 sts, invdec* 6 times (30 sts).

Rnd 21: *sc in next 3 sts, invdec* 6 times (24 sts).

Rnd 22: *sc in next 2 sts, invdec* 6 times (18 sts).

Rnd 23: *sc in next st, invdec* 6 times (12 sts).

Rnd 24: invdec 6 times (6 sts).

Fasten off. Finish adding stuffing.

To close hole, thread tail in yarn needle, insert needle thru front loop of each st around opening and pull tight. Weave in end.

Squeeze Head into shape.

TURBAN RING

With purple yarn, make a magic ring, ch 1.

Rnd 1: 7 sc in ring, pull ring closed tight (7 sts).

Rnds 2-?: sc in each st around until tube is long enough to wrap around head where color changes from brown to lavender.

Sl st in next st. Fasten off.

FINISHING

Wrap Turban Ring around Head and glue in place as pictured: insert pins to hold in place until glue dries. With yarn tails, whip st ends of Turban Ring together. Hide tails inside Head. Glue on jewels.

Glue on eyes between Rnds 13-14 with an interspace of 7-8 sts.

With brown yarn, embroider nose 2 rows below eyes.

Attach jump ring (see page 80).

Ox

SUPPLIES

G6/4mm crochet hook

Worsted weight yarn in rust, beige and black

2 black safety eyes, 8mm

Polyester fiberfill stuffing

Jump ring, 10mm

Note: A ch 1 at the beginning of a rnd is for turning your work and does not count as a st.

HEAD

With beige yarn, make a magic ring, ch 1.

Rnd 1: 6 sc in ring, pull ring closed tight (6 sts).

Rnd 2: *3 sc in next st, 2 sc in next st, sc in next st* twice. Place marker for beginning of rnd and move marker up as each rnd is completed (12 sts).

Rnd 3: sc in next st, 2 sc in next 3 sts, sc in next 3 sts, 2 sc in next 3 sts, sc in next 2 sts (18 sts).

Rnd 4: sc in next 2 sts, 2 sc in next st, *sc in next st, 2 sc in next st* twice, sc in next 4 sts, 2 sc in next st, *sc in next st, 2 sc in next st* twice, sc in next 2 sts; change to rust yarn in last st (24 sts).

Rnd 5: sl st loosely in first st, sc in each remaining st around (24 sts).

Rnd 6: *sc in next 3 sts, 2 sc in next st* 6 times (30 sts).

Rnd 7: sc in each st around.

Rnd 8: *sc in next 4 sts, 2 sc in next st* 6 times (36 sts).

Rnds 9-13: sc in each st around.

Rnd 14: *sc in next 4 sts, invdec* 6 times (30 sts).

Rnd 15: *sc in next 3 sts, invdec* 6 times (24 sts).

Start to stuff and continue stuffing after each rnd.

Rnd 16: *sc in next 2 sts, invdec* 6 times (18 sts).

Rnd 17: *sc in next st, invdec* 6 times (12 sts).

Rnd 18: invdec 6 times (6 sts).

Fasten off. Finish adding stuffing.

To close hole, thread tail in yarn needle, insert needle thru front loop of each st around opening and pull tight. Weave in end.

Squeeze Head into shape so that it is rounded at the back and tapered toward the snout.

HORNS (MAKE 2)

With beige yarn, make a magic ring, ch 1.

Rnd 1: 4 sc in ring, pull ring closed tight (4 sts).

Rnd 2: sc in next 3 sts, 2 sc in next st (5 sts).

Rnd 3: sc in next 4 sts, 2 sc in next st (6 sts).

Rnds 4-5: sc in each st around. Fasten off.

EARS (MAKE 2)

The ears are worked around a foundation chain.

EAR FRONT

With beige yarn, ch 5.

Rnd 1: starting in 2nd ch from hook, sc in next 3 chs, 3 sc in last ch, sc in next 3 ch (9 sts).

Rnd 2: ch 1, turn, sc in next 4 sts, 3 sc in next st, sc in next 4 sts (11 sts). Fasten off.

EAR BACK

With rust yarn, ch 5.

Rnd 1: starting in 2nd ch from hook, sc in next 3 chs, 3 sc in last ch, sc in next 3 ch (9 sts).

Rnd 2: ch 1, turn, sc in next 4 sts, 3 sc in next st, sc in next 4 sts (11 sts).

Rnd 3: ch 1, turn, place Ear Front against Ear Back with wrong sides facing and sts aligned. Working thru both layers, sc in next 5 sts, 3 sc in next st, sc in next 5 sts (13 sts).

Rnd 4: ch 1, turn, sc in next 6 sts, 3 sc in next st, sc in next 6 sts (15 sts). Fasten off.

Sew first 3 tails into space between layers of Ear to hide them, cut off excess.

Thread remaining tail in yarn needle, sew into opposite corner and pull tight. This will connect the corners and shape the Ear. Secure with a stitch and knot.

Pinch tip of Ear into a point.

FINISHING

Orient Head as shown in picture so that beige oval (snout area) is positioned in a horizontal direction.

Glue on eyes between Rnds 8-9 with an interspace of 7-8 sts.

Sew Horns and Ears to top of Head as shown in picture.

With a double strand of black yarn, embroider nostrils.

For forehead fringe, cut five 4" pieces of rust yarn. Attach each strand to top of Head as follows: Insert hook thru a st. Pull center of strand part way thru st to make a loop. Feed ends of yarn thru loop and pull loop tight. Trim ends if desired.

Attach jump ring (see page 80).

Donkey

SUPPLIES

G6/4mm crochet hook

Worsted weight yarn in light gray, medium gray and black

2 black safety eyes, 8mm

Glue (see page 8)

Polyester fiberfill stuffing

Jump ring, 10mm

Note: A chain 1 at the beginning of a rnd is for turning your work and does not count as a stitch.

HEAD

With light gray yarn, make a magic ring, ch 1.

Rnd 1: 6 sc in ring, pull ring closed tight (6 sts).

Rnd 2: *3 sc in next st, 2 sc in next st, sc in next st* twice. Place marker for beginning of rnd and move marker up as each rnd is completed (12 sts).

Rnd 3: sc in next st, 2 sc in next 3 sts, sc in next 3 sts, 2 sc in next 3 sts, sc in next 2 sts (18 sts).

Rnd 4: sc in next 2 sts, 2 sc in next st, *sc in next st, 2 sc in next st* twice, sc in next 4 sts, 2 sc in next st, *sc in next st, 2 sc in next st* twice, sc in next 2 sts; change to medium gray yarn in last st (24 sts).

Rnd 5: sl st loosely in first st, sc in each remaining st around (24 sts).

Rnd 6: *sc in next 3 sts, 2 sc in next st* 6 times (30 sts).

Rnd 7: sc in each st around.

Rnd 8: *sc in next 4 sts, 2 sc in next st* 6 times (36 sts).

Rnds 9-13: sc in each st around.

Rnd 14: *sc in next 4 sts, invdec* 6 times (30 sts).

Rnd 15: *sc in next 3 sts, invdec* 6 times (24 sts).

Start to stuff and continue stuffing after each rnd.

Rnd 16: *sc in next 2 sts, invdec* 6 times (18 sts).

Rnd 17: *sc in next st, invdec* 6 times (12 sts).

Rnd 18: invdec 6 times (6 sts).

Fasten off. Finish adding stuffing.

To close hole, thread tail in yarn needle, insert needle thru front loop of each st around opening and pull tight. Weave in end.

Squeeze Head into shape so that it is rounded at the back and tapered toward the snout.

EARS (MAKE 2)

The ears are worked around a foundation chain.

EAR FRONT

With light gray yarn, ch 7.

Rnd 1: starting in 2nd ch from hook, sc in next 5 chs, 3 sc in last ch, sc in next 5 ch (13 sts). Fasten off.

EAR BACK

With medium gray yarn, ch 7.

Rnd 1: starting in 2nd ch from hook, sc in next 5 chs, 3 sc in last ch, sc in next 5 ch (13 sts).

Rnd 2: ch 1, turn, place Ear Front against Ear Back with wrong sides facing and sts aligned. Working thru both layers, sc in next 6 sts, 3 sc in next st, sc in next 6 sts (15 sts).

Rnd 3: ch 1, turn, sc in next 7 sts, 3 sc in next st, sc in next 7 sts (17 sts).

Rnd 4: ch 1, turn, sc in next 8 sts, 3 sc in next st, sc in next 8 sts (19 sts). Fasten off.

Sew first 3 tails into space between layers of Ear to hide them, cut off excess. Thread remaining tail in yarn needle, sew into opposite corner and pull tight. This will connect the corners and shape the Ear. Secure with a stitch and knot.

FINISHING

Orient Head as shown in picture so that light gray oval (snout area) is positioned in a vertical direction.

Glue on eyes between Rnds 7-8 with an interspace of 7-8 sts.

Sew Ears to top of Head as shown in picture.

With a double strand of black yarn, embroider nostrils.

For forehead fringe, cut five 4" pieces of black yarn. Attach each strand to top of Head as follows: Insert hook thru a st. Pull center of strand part way thru st to make a loop. Feed ends of yarn thru loop and pull loop tight. Trim ends if desired.

Attach jump ring (see page 80).

SHEEP

Loop stitch (lp st) is used to make the Sheep's cap of curly fleece. See page 77 if you're unfamiliar with this stitch. You may also want to visit YouTube to watch a video demo.

SUPPLIES

G6/4mm crochet hook

Worsted weight yarn in cream, pink and black

2 black safety eyes, 8mm

Glue (see page 8)

Polyester fiberfill stuffing

Jump ring, 10mm

Note: A ch 1 at the beginning of a rnd is for turning your work and does not count as a st.

HEAD

With cream yarn, make a magic ring, ch 1.

Rnd 1: 6 sc in ring, pull ring closed tight (6 sts).

Rnd 2: 2 sc in each st around. Place marker for beginning of rnd and move marker up as each rnd is completed (12 sts).

Rnd 3: *sc in next st, 2 sc in next st* 6 times (18 sts).

Rnd 4: sc in each st around.

Rnd 5: *sc in next 2 sts, 2 sc in next st* 6 times (24 sts).

Rnd 6: sc in each st around.

Rnd 7: *sc in next 3 sts, 2 sc in next st* 6 times (30 sts).

Rnd 8: sc in each st around.

Rnd 9: *sc in next 4 sts, 2 sc in next st* 6 times (36 sts).

Rnds 10-14: sc in each st around.

Start to stuff and continue stuffing after each rnd.

Rnd 15: *sc in next 4 sts, invdec* 6 times (30 sts).

Rnd 16: *sc in next 3 sts, invdec* 6 times (24 sts).

Rnd 17: *sc in next 2 sts, invdec* 6 times (18 sts).

Rnd 18: *sc in next st, invdec* 6 times (12 sts).

Rnd 19: invdec 6 times (6 sts).

Fasten off. Finish adding stuffing.

To close hole, thread tail in yarn needle, insert needle thru front loop of each st around opening and pull tight. Weave in end. Squeeze Head into shape.

CURLY CAP

With cream yarn, make a magic ring, ch 1.

Rnd 1: 6 sc in ring, pull ring closed tight (6 sts).

The remaining rnds are worked **in back loops only.**

Rnd 2: 2 lp st in each st around. Place marker for beginning of rnd and move marker up as each rnd is completed (12 sts).

Rnd 3: *lp st in next st, 2 lp st in next st* 6 times (18 sts).

Rnd 4: *lp st in next 2 sts, 2 lp st in next st* 6 times (24 sts).

Rnd 5: *lp st in next 3 sts, 2 lp st in next st* 6 times (30 sts).

Rnd 6: *lp st in next 4 sts, 2 lp st in next st* 6 times (36 sts).

Rnds 7-11: lp st in each st around. Fasten off.

EARS (MAKE 2)

The Ears are worked around a foundation chain.

EAR FRONT

With pink yarn, ch 5.

Rnd 1: starting in 2nd ch from hook, sc in next 3 chs, 3 sc in last ch, sc in next 3 ch (9 sts).

Rnd 2: ch 1, turn, sc in next 4 sts, 3 sc in next st, sc in next 4 sts (11 sts). Fasten off.

EAR BACK

With cream yarn, ch 5.

Rnd 1: starting in 2nd ch from hook, sc in next 3 chs, 3 sc in last ch, sc in next 3 ch (9 sts).

Rnd 2: ch 1, turn, sc in next 4 sts, 3 sc in next st, sc in next 4 sts (11 sts).

Rnd 3: ch 1, turn, place Ear Front against Ear Back with wrong sides facing and sts aligned. Working thru both layers, sc in next 5 sts, 3 sc in next st, sc in next 5 sts (13 sts).

Rnd 4: ch 1, turn, sc in next 6 sts, 3 sc in next st, sc in next 6 sts (15 sts). Fasten off.

Sew first 3 tails into space between layers of Ear to hide them, cut off excess. Thread remaining tail in yarn needle, sew into opposite corner and pull tight. This will connect the corners and shape the Ear. Secure with a stitch and knot.

Pinch tip of Ear into a point.

FINISHING

Glue Curly Cap to Head so that Rnd 1 of Cap meets Rnd 19 of Head.

Glue on eyes between Rnds 7-8 with an interspace of 7-8 sts.

Separate loops to make spaces for Ears and sew on Ears as shown in picture.

With a double strand of black yarn, embroider a Y at center front.

Attach jump ring (see page 80).

North Pole Characters

Santa Claus

SUPPLIES

G6/4mm crochet hook

Worsted weight yarn in beige, red and white

2 black safety eyes, 8mm

Glue (see page 8)

Polyester fiberfill stuffing

Jump ring, 10mm

HEAD

With white yarn, make a magic ring, ch 1.

Rnd 1: 6 sc in ring, pull ring closed tight (6 sts).

Rnd 2: *sc in next st, 2 sc in next st* 3 times. Place marker for beginning of rnd and move marker up as each rnd is completed (9 sts).

Rnd 3: *sc in next 2 sts, 2 sc in next st* 3 times (12 sts).

Rnd 4: *sc in next 2 sts, 2 sc in next st* 4 times (16 sts).

Rnd 5: *sc in next 3 sts, 2 sc in next st* 4 times (20 sts).

Rnd 6: *sc in next 4 sts, 2 sc in next st* 4 times (24 sts).

Rnd 7: *sc in next 5 sts, 2 sc in next st* 4 times (28 sts).

Rnd 8: *sc in next 6 sts, 2 sc in next st* 4 times (32 sts).

Rnd 9: *sc in next 7 sts, 2 sc in next st* 4 times; change to beige yarn in last st (36 sts).

Rnds 10-15: sc in each st around; change to red yarn in last st.

Rnds 16-19: sc in each st around.

Rnd 20: *sc in next 4 sts, invdec* 6 times (30 sts).

Rnd 21: sc in each st around.

Rnd 22: *sc in next st, invdec* 10 times (20 sts).

Rnds 23-24: sc in each st around.

Stuff the Head.

Rnd 25: *sc in next 2 sts, invdec* 5 times (15 sts).

Rnds 26-28: sc in each st around.

Rnd 29: *sc in next st, invdec* 5 times (10 sts).

Rnds 30-35: sc in each st around.

Fasten off. Finish adding stuffing if needed. The stuffing should only go thru Rnd 24. The tip that gets bent doesn't get stuffed.

To close hole, thread tail in yarn needle, insert needle thru front loop of each st around opening and pull tight. Weave in end.

Squeeze Head into shape.

HAT BAND

With white yarn, ch 45.

Rows 1-2: ch 1, turn, sc in each ch across (45 sts).

Fasten off.

BALL

With white yarn, make a magic ring, ch 1.

Rnd 1: 6 sc in ring, pull ring closed tight (6 sts).

Rnd 2: 2 sc in each st around. Place marker for beginning of rnd and move marker up as each rnd is completed (12 sts).

Rnds 3-4: sc in each st around.

Rnd 5: invdec 6 times (6 sts).

Fasten off. Stuff Ball.

To close hole, thread tail in yarn needle, insert needle thru front loop of each st around opening and pull tight.

FINISHING

Glue on eyes between Rnds 13-14 with an interspace of 7-8 sts.

With red yarn, embroider nose 2 rows below eyes.

Glue Hat Band wrong side out around Head where beige yarn changes to red. With yarn tails, whip st ends of Hat Band together. Hide tails inside Head.

Bend narrow red end of Head downward to form Santa's hat and sew in place as pictured. Sew Ball to tip.

Attach jump ring (see page 80).

MRS. CLAUS

The lovely poinsettia is made with DK, Light Worsted yarn. Embroidered French Knots can be substituted for the yellow beads if desired.

SUPPLIES

F5/3.75mm and G6/4mm crochet hooks

DK, Light Worsted yarn in red and green

Worsted weight yarn in beige and gray

2 black safety eyes, 8mm

5 yellow beads, 4mm

Sewing thread

Glue (see page 8)

Polyester fiberfill stuffing

Jump ring, 10mm

HEAD

With G6/4mm crochet hook and gray yarn, make a magic ring, ch 1.

Rnd 1: 6 sc in ring, pull ring closed tight (6 sts).

Rnd 2: 2 sc in each st around. Place marker for beginning of rnd and move marker up as each rnd is completed (12 sts).

Rnd 3: *sc in next st, 2 sc in next st* 6 times (18 sts).

Rnd 4: *sc in next 2 sts, 2 sc in next st* 6 times (24 sts).

Rnd 5: *sc in next 3 sts, 2 sc in next st* 6 times (30 sts).

Rnd 6: *sc in next 4 sts, 2 sc in next st* 6 times (36 sts).

Rnds 7-9: sc in each st around; change to beige yarn in last st.

Rnds 10-13: sc in each st around.

Rnd 14: *sc in next 4 sts, invdec* 6 times (30 sts).

Rnd 15: *sc in next 3 sts, invdec* 6 times (24 sts).

Start to stuff and continue stuffing after each rnd.

Rnd 16: *sc in next 2 sts, invdec* 6 times (18 sts).

Rnd 17: *sc in next st, invdec* 6 times (12 sts).

Rnd 18: invdec 6 times (6 sts).

Fasten off. Finish adding stuffing.

To close hole, thread tail in yarn needle, insert needle thru front loop of each st around opening and pull tight. Weave in end.

Squeeze Head into a nice round shape.

BUN

With gray yarn, make a magic ring, ch 1.

Rnd 1: 6 sc in ring, pull ring closed tight (6 sts).

Rnd 2: 2 sc in each st around. Place marker for beginning of rnd and move marker up as each rnd is completed (12 sts).

Rnd 3: *sc in next st, 2 sc in next st* 6 times (18 sts).

Rnds 4-6: sc in each st around.

Rnd 7: *sc in next st, invdec* 6 times (12 sts).

Fasten off. Stuff the Bun.

SMALL PETALS (MAKE 5)

The Petals are worked around a foundation chain.

With F5/3.75mm crochet hook and red yarn, ch 8 loosely.

Rnd 1: sc in 2nd ch from hook, hdc in next ch, dc in next 3 ch, hdc in next ch, 3 sc in end ch, hdc in next ch, dc in next 3 ch, hdc in next ch, sc in next ch, sl st in 1st ch. Place marker at beginning of rnd (16 sts). Fasten off. Weave in ends.

LARGE PETALS (MAKE 5)

With G6/4mm crochet hook, follow instructions for Small Petals.

LEAVES (MAKE 3)

With G6/4mm crochet hook and green yarn, follow instructions for Small Petals.

FINISHING

Glue on eyes between Rnds 11-12 with an interspace of 7-8 sts.

With beige yarn, embroider nose 2 rows below eyes.

Sew Bun to top of Head.

String Small Petals together by running a piece of red yarn on a yarn needle thru base (rounded end) of each Petal. Knot yarn ends together to make a ring of Petals. Repeat with Large Petals.

Stack Small Petals on Large Petals with Petals staggered; glue rings together with a circle of glue close to the center.

Sew beads to center of flower.

Sew flower to Head as shown in picture.

Tuck Leaves under Petals and sew or glue in place as shown in picture.

Attach jump ring (see page 80).

REINDEER

SUPPLIES

G6/4mm crochet hook

Worsted weight yarn in tan, white, brown and red

2 black safety eyes, 8mm

Glue (see page 8)

Polyester fiberfill stuffing

Jump ring, 10mm

Note: A ch 1 at the beginning of a rnd is for turning your work and does not count as a st.

HEAD

With red yarn, make a magic ring, ch 1.

Rnd 1: 6 sc in ring, pull ring closed tight, join with sl st in first st; change to white yarn in the sl st (6 sts).

Rnd 2: *sc in next st, 2 sc in next st* 3 times. Place marker for beginning of rnd and move marker up as each rnd is completed (9 sts).

Rnd 3: *sc in next 2 sts, 2 sc in next st* 3 times (12 sts).

Rnd 4: *sc in next 2 sts, 2 sc in next st* 4 times (16 sts).

Rnd 5: *sc in next 3 sts, 2 sc in next st* 4 times; change to tan yarn in last st (20 sts).

Rnd 6: *sc in next 4 sts, 2 sc in next st* 4 times (24 sts).

Rnd 7: *sc in next 5 sts, 2 sc in next st* 4 times (28 sts).

Rnd 8: *sc in next 6 sts, 2 sc in next st* 4 times (32 sts).

Rnd 9: *sc in next 7 sts, 2 sc in next st* 4 times (36 sts).

Rnds 10-16: sc in each st around.

Start to stuff and continue stuffing after each round.

Rnd 17: *sc in next 4 sts, invdec* 6 times (30 sts).

Rnd 18: *sc in next 3 sts, invdec* 6 times (24 sts).

Rnd 19: *sc in next 2 sts, invdec* 6 times (18 sts).

Rnd 20: *sc in next st, invdec* 6 times (12 sts).

Rnd 21: invdec 6 times (6 sts).

Fasten off. Finish adding stuffing.

To close hole, thread tail in yarn needle, insert needle thru front loop of each st around opening and pull tight. Weave in end.

Squeeze Head into shape.

EARS (MAKE 2)

The ears are worked around a foundation chain.

EAR FRONT

With white yarn, ch 5.

Rnd 1: starting in 2nd ch from hook, sc in next 3 chs, 3 sc in last ch, sc in next 3 ch (9 sts).

Rnd 2: ch 1, turn, sc in next 4 sts, 3 sc in next st, sc in next 4 sts (11 sts). Fasten off.

EAR BACK

With tan yarn, ch 5.

Rnd 1: starting in 2nd ch from hook, sc in next 3 chs, 3 sc in last ch, sc in next 3 ch (9 sts).

Rnd 2: ch 1, turn, sc in next 4 sts, 3 sc in next st, sc in next 4 sts (11 sts).

Rnd 3: ch 1, turn, place Ear Front against Ear Back with wrong sides facing and sts aligned. Working thru both layers, sc in next 5 sts, 3 sc in next st, sc in next 5 sts (13 sts).

Rnd 4: ch 1, turn, sc in next 6 sts, 3 sc in next st, sc in next 6 sts (15 sts). Fasten off.

Sew first 3 tails into space between layers of Ear to hide them, cut off excess. Thread remaining tail in yarn needle, sew into opposite corner and pull tight. This will connect the corners and shape the Ear. Secure with a stitch and knot.

Pinch tip of Ear into a point.

ANTLERS (MAKE 2)

The Antlers are made in 2 parts.

Part A

With brown yarn, make a magic ring, ch 1.

Rnd 1: 6 sc in ring, pull ring closed tight (6 sts).

Rnds 2-?: sc in each st around until piece is 2 1/2" long.

Fasten off.

Part B

With brown yarn, make a magic ring, ch 1.

Rnd 1: 6 sc in ring, pull ring closed tight (6 sts).

Rnds 2-?: sc in each st around until piece is 1" long.

Fasten off.

Sew Parts A and B together as shown in picture.

FINISHING

Glue on eyes between Rnds 10-11 with an interspace of 7-8 sts.

Embroider eye rims with a double strand of white yarn.

Sew Antlers on Rnds 15-16 of Head. Sew an Ear beside each Antler.

Attach jump ring (see page 80).

ELF

SUPPLIES

G6/4mm crochet hook

Worsted weight yarn in beige, brown, green, red and gold

2 black safety eyes, 8mm

14 gold beads, 3mm

Sewing thread

Glue (see page 8)

Polyester fiberfill stuffing

Jump ring, 10mm

Note: A ch 1 at the beginning of a row is for turning your work and does not count as a st.

HEAD

With green yarn, make a magic ring, ch 1.

Rnd 1: 6 sc in ring, pull ring closed tight (6 sts).

Rnd 2: *sc in next st, 2 sc in next st* 3 times. Place marker for beginning of rnd and move marker up as each rnd is completed (9 sts).

Rnd 3: *sc in next 2 sts, 2 sc in next st* 3 times (12 sts).

Rnd 4: *sc in next 2 sts, 2 sc in next st* 4 times (16 sts).

Rnd 5: *sc in next 3 sts, 2 sc in next st* 4 times (20 sts).

Rnd 6: *sc in next 4 sts, 2 sc in next st* 4 times (24 sts).

Rnd 7: *sc in next 5 sts, 2 sc in next st* 4 times (28 sts).

Rnd 8: *sc in next 6 sts, 2 sc in next st* 4 times (32 sts).

Rnd 9: *sc in next 7 sts, 2 sc in next st* 4 times (36 sts).

Rnds 10-12: sc in each st around; change to brown yarn in last st.

Rnd 13: sc in each st around, join with sl st in first st; change to beige yarn in the sl st (36 sts).

Rnds 14-19: sc in each st around.

Start to stuff and continue stuffing after each rnd.

Rnd 20: *sc in next 4 sts, invdec* 6 times (30 sts).

Rnd 21: *sc in next 3 sts, invdec* 6 times (24 sts).

Rnd 22: *sc in next 2 sts, invdec* 6 times (18 sts).

Rnd 23: *sc in next st, invdec* 6 times (12 sts).

Rnd 24: invdec 6 times (6 sts).

Fasten off. Finish adding stuffing.

To close hole, thread tail in yarn needle, insert needle thru front loop of each st around opening and pull tight. Weave in end. Squeeze Head into shape.

BALL

With gold yarn, make a magic ring, ch 1.

Rnd 1: 4 sc in ring, pull ring closed tight (4 sts).

Rnd 2: 2 sc in each st around. Place marker for beginning of rnd and move marker up as each rnd is completed (8 sts).

Rnds 3-4: sc in each st around.

Rnd 5: invdec 4 times (4 sts). Fasten off. Stuff Ball.

HAT BAND

With green yarn, ch 41.

Row 1: pull up a loop of red yarn, ch 1, turn, sc in each st across (41 sts).

Row 2: ch 1, turn, sc in first st, *ch 3 loosely, sl st in back bar of 3rd ch from hook, skip 1 st, sc in next 2 sts* 13 times, sc in last st. Fasten off.

FINISHING

Glue on eyes between Rnds 15-16 with an interspace of 7-8 sts.

With beige yarn, embroider nose 2 rows below eyes.

Sew beads to points of Hat Band.

Glue Hat Band wrong side out around Head where green yarn changes to brown leaving a visible fringe of brown for bangs. With yarn tails, whip st ends of Hat Band together. Hide tails inside Head.

Sew Ball to top as shown in picture.

Attach jump ring (see page 80).

Snowman

An optional cardboard lining can be placed in the Hat to keep it in shape.

SUPPLIES

G6/4mm crochet hook

Worsted weight yarn in white, black, blue and orange

2 black safety eyes, 8mm

Glue (see page 8)

Lightweight cardboard such as cereal box (optional)

Stapler (optional)

Polyester fiberfill stuffing

Jump ring, 10mm

HEAD

With white yarn, make a magic ring, ch 1.

Rnd 1: 6 sc in ring, pull ring closed tight (6 sts).

Rnd 2: 2 sc in each st around. Place marker for beginning of rnd and move marker up as each rnd is completed (12 sts).

Rnd 3: *sc in next st, 2 sc in next st* 6 times (18 sts).

Rnd 4: *sc in next 2 sts, 2 sc in next st* 6 times (24 sts).

Rnd 5: *sc in next 3 sts, 2 sc in next st* 6 times (30 sts).

Rnd 6: *sc in next 4 sts, 2 sc in next st* 6 times (36 sts).

Rnds 7-13: sc in each st around.

Rnd 14: *sc in next 4 sts, invdec* 6 times (30 sts).

Rnd 15: *sc in next 3 sts, invdec* 6 times (24 sts).

Start to stuff and continue stuffing after each rnd.

Rnd 16: *sc in next 2 sts, invdec* 6 times (18 sts).

Rnd 17: *sc in next st, invdec* 6 times (12 sts).

Rnd 18: invdec 6 times (6 sts).

Fasten off. Finish adding stuffing.

To close hole, thread tail in yarn needle, insert needle thru front loop of each st around opening and pull tight. Weave in end.

Squeeze Head into a nice round shape.

HAT

With black yarn, make a magic ring, ch 1.

Rnd 1: 6 sc in ring, pull ring closed tight (6 sts).

Rnd 2: 2 sc in each st around. Place marker for beginning of rnd and move marker up as each rnd is completed (12 sts).

Rnd 3: *sc in next st, 2 sc in next st* 6 times (18 sts).

Rnd 4: *sc in next 2 sts, 2 sc in next st* 6 times (24 sts).

Rnd 5: *sc in next 3 sts, 2 sc in next st* 6 times (30 sts).

Rnd 6: *sc in next 4 sts, 2 sc in next st* 6 times (36 sts).

Rnd 7: *sc in next 5 sts, 2 sc in next st* 6 times (42 sts).

Rnd 8: working in **back loops** only, sc in each st around.

Rnds 9-13: resuming work in **both loops,** sc in each st around; change to blue yarn in last st.

Rnds 14-15: sc in each st around; change to black yarn in last st.

Rnd 16: working in **front loops** only, *sc in next 6 sts, 2 sc in next st* 6 times (48 sts).

Rnd 17: resuming work in **both loops**, *sc in next 7 sts, 2 sc in next st* 6 times (54 sts).

Rnd 18: *sc in next 8 sts, 2 sc in next st* 6 times (60 sts).

Rnd 19: sl st in each st around. Fasten off.

FINISHING

Glue on eyes between Rnds 9-10 with an interspace of 7-8 sts.

With orange yarn, embroider nose 2 rows below eyes.

Optional: For cardboard lining in Hat, cut a circle of cardboard using Hat Template on page 38 and a strip of cardboard measuring ~1.25" x 10". Coil strip into a ring and place inside Hat to check fit. (Keep edge slightly above bottom of Hat to allow for sewing.) When fit is good, secure shape with staples. Glue circle to inside/top of Hat. Nest ring inside Hat.

Stuff Hat lightly and place over final rnds of Head. Sew Hat to Head as shown in picture.

Attach jump ring (see page 80).

Gingerbread Man

The Gingerbread Man has a cap of frosting with embroidered sprinkles. Bugle beads can be glued on for sprinkles if preferred.

SUPPLIES

G6/4mm crochet hook

Worsted weight yarn in honey, white, red and green

2 black safety eyes, 8mm

Glue (see page 8)

Polyester fiberfill stuffing

Jump ring, 10mm

HEAD

With white yarn, make a magic ring, ch 1.

Rnd 1: 6 sc in ring, pull ring closed tight (6 sts).

Rnd 2: 2 sc in each st around. Place marker for beginning of rnd and move marker up as each rnd is completed (12 sts).

Rnd 3: *sc in next st, 2 sc in next st* 6 times (18 sts).

Rnd 4: *sc in next 2 sts, 2 sc in next st* 6 times (24 sts).

Rnd 5: *sc in next 3 sts, 2 sc in next st* 6 times (30 sts).

Rnd 6: *sc in next 4 sts, 2 sc in next st* 6 times (36 sts).

Rnds 7-9: sc in each st around; change to honey yarn in last st.

Rnd 10: working in **back loops only**, sc in each st around.

Rnds 11-13: resuming work **in both loops,** sc in each st around.

Rnd 14: *sc in next 4 sts, invdec* 6 times (30 sts).

Rnd 15: *sc in next 3 sts, invdec* 6 times (24 sts).

Start to stuff and continue stuffing after each rnd.

Rnd 16: *sc in next 2 sts, invdec* 6 times (18 sts).

Rnd 17: *sc in next st, invdec* 6 times (12 sts).

Rnd 18: invdec 6 times (6 sts).

Fasten off. Finish adding stuffing.

To close hole, thread tail in yarn needle, insert needle thru front loop of each st around opening and pull tight. Weave in end.

Squeeze Head into a nice round shape.

SCALLOPED EDGE

Hold Head with white side facing you. Join white yarn with sl st at center back in unworked front loop of Rnd 10.

Rnd 1: (sc, dc, sc) in next st, sl st in next st, *sl st in next st, (sc, dc, sc) in next st, sl st in next st* 11 times (12 scallops).

Fasten off. Weave in end.

CHERRY

With red yarn, make a magic ring, ch 1.

Rnd 1: 4 sc in ring, pull ring closed tight (4 sts).

Rnd 2: 2 sc in each st around. Place marker for beginning of rnd and move marker up as each rnd is completed (8 sts).

Rnds 3-4: sc in each st around.

Rnd 5: invdec 4 times (4 sts).

Fasten off. Stuff Cherry.

FINISHING

Glue on eyes between Rnds 12-13 with an interspace of 7-8 sts.

With green yarn, embroider nose 2 rows below eyes.

With red and green yarn, embroider sprinkles as shown in picture.

Attach jump ring (see page 80).

Toy Soldier

An optional cardboard lining in the Hat will keep it in perfect shape.

SUPPLIES

G6/4mm crochet hook

Worsted weight yarn in beige, blue, yellow, red, white and black

2 black safety eyes, 8mm

1 metallic button, 7/8"

1 acrylic craft jewel in red

Sewing thread

Glue (see page 8)

Lightweight cardboard such as cereal box (optional)

Stapler (optional)

Polyester fiberfill stuffing

Jump ring, 10mm

HEAD

With beige yarn, make a magic ring, ch 1.

Rnd 1: 6 sc in ring, pull ring closed tight (6 sts).

Rnd 2: 2 sc in each st around. Place marker for beginning of rnd and move marker up as each rnd is completed (12 sts).

Rnd 3: *sc in next st, 2 sc in next st* 6 times (18 sts).

Rnd 4: *sc in next 2 sts, 2 sc in next st* 6 times (24 sts).

Rnd 5: *sc in next 3 sts, 2 sc in next st* 6 times (30 sts).

Rnd 6: *sc in next 4 sts, 2 sc in next st* 6 times (36 sts).

Rnds 7-13: sc in each st around.

Rnd 14: *sc in next 4 sts, invdec* 6 times (30 sts).

Rnd 15: *sc in next 3 sts, invdec* 6 times (24 sts).

Start to stuff and continue stuffing after each rnd.

Rnd 16: *sc in next 2 sts, invdec* 6 times (18 sts).

Rnd 17: *sc in next st, invdec* 6 times (12 sts).

Rnd 18: invdec 6 times (6 sts).

Fasten off. Finish adding stuffing.

To close hole, thread tail in yarn needle, insert needle thru front loop of each st around opening and pull tight. Weave in end.

Squeeze Head into a nice round shape.

FEATHER

The Feather is worked around a foundation chain.

With yellow yarn, ch 8 loosely.

Rnd 1: sc in 2nd ch from hook, hdc in next ch, dc in next 3 ch, hdc in next ch, 3 sc in end ch, hdc in next ch, dc in next 3 ch, hdc in next ch, sc in next ch, sl st in 1st ch. Place marker at beginning of rnd (16 sts). Fasten off. Weave in ends

HAT

With blue yarn, make a magic ring, ch 1.

Rnd 1: 6 sc in ring, pull ring closed tight (6 sts).

Rnd 2: 2 sc in each st around. Place marker for beginning of rnd and move marker up as each rnd is completed (12 sts).

Rnd 3: *sc in next st, 2 sc in next st* 6 times (18 sts).

Rnd 4: *sc in next 2 sts, 2 sc in next st* 6 times (24 sts).

Rnd 5: *sc in next 3 sts, 2 sc in next st* 6 times (30 sts).

Rnd 6: *sc in next 4 sts, 2 sc in next st* 6 times (36 sts).

Rnd 7: *sc in next 5 sts, 2 sc in next st* 6 times (42 sts).

Rnd 8: working in **back loops only**, sc in each st around.

Rnds 9-16: resuming work in **both loops**, sc in each st around; change to yellow yarn in last st.

Rnd 17: sc in each st around; change to blue yarn in last st.

Rnd 18: sc in each st around. Fasten off.

For **Visor,** count 13 sts from where you fastened off Rnd 18 and join red yarn with sl st, sl st in next st, sc in next 2 sts, hdc in next 2 sts, dc in next 6 sts, hdc in next 2 sts, sc in next 2 sts, sl st in next 2 sts. Fasten off. Weave in ends.

For **Chin Strap,** join black yarn with sl st at one edge of Visor. Chain 25. Join with sl st at other edge of Visor using care not to twist the chain. Fasten off.

For **Cord,** ch 26 with white yarn. Fasten off. Sew tails thru groove between Rnds 9-10 as shown in picture. Weave in ends.

For **Ornament,** glue jewel to center of button; stack on top of Feather and sew to Hat as shown in picture.

FINISHING

Glue on eyes between Rnds 9-10 with an interspace of 7-8 sts.

With red yarn, embroider nose 2 rows below eyes.

Optional: For cardboard lining in Hat, cut a circle of cardboard using Hat Template below and a strip of cardboard measuring ~2" x 10". Coil strip into a ring and place inside Hat to check fit. (Be sure edge is slightly above bottom of Hat to allow for sewing.) When fit is good, secure shape with staples. Glue circle to inside/top of Hat. Nest ring inside Hat.

Stuff Hat and sew to Head as shown in picture.

Attach jump ring (see page 80).

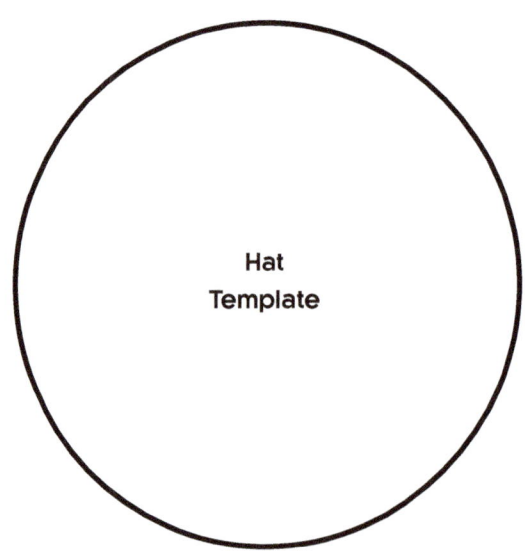

Hat Template

Sweet Treats

Candy Cane

This easy pattern consists of a 4-row striped rectangle that is coiled around a wire core and sewn in place.

SUPPLIES

G6/4mm crochet hook

Worsted weight yarn in red and white

2 chenille pipe cleaners

1 piece of 18-gauge floral stem wire

Sewing thread in white

Needle-nose pliers

Jump ring, 10mm

Note: A ch 1 at the beginning of a row is for turning your work and does not count as a st.

With white yarn, ch 51.

Row 1: sc in 2nd ch from hook and in each remaining ch across; change to red yarn in last st (50 sts).

Rows 2-3: ch 1, turn, sc in each st across; change to white yarn in last st.

Row 4: ch 1, turn, sc in each st across. Fasten off.

FINISHING

With pliers, bend a small loop at one end of stem wire to conceal sharp tip. Use this as your top end. Hold stem wire and pipe cleaners together in a bundle to form Candy Cane's core.

Lay wire bundle on wrong side of fabric 1/2" from top edge. Fold right corner down to meet left edge (see Fig. A).

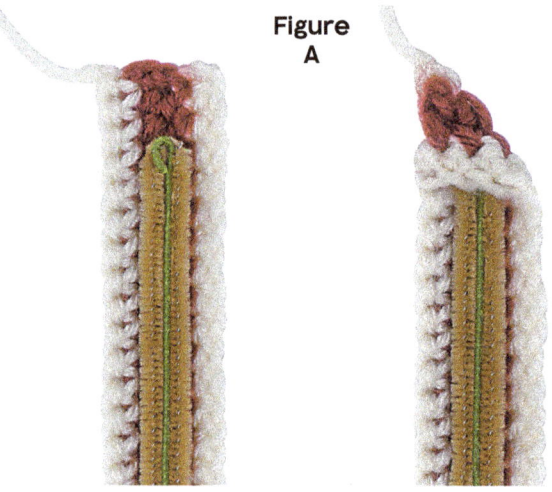

Figure A

Coil fabric in a spiral course around core until all fabric is wrapped & core is covered (see Fig. B). Cut off excess length of pipe cleaners & cut off floral wire with 1/4" extra. Bend a small loop in lower end of floral wire to conceal sharp tip.

Figure B

With sewing needle and thread, sew edges together. When sewing across ends, make a stitch thru loops in top and bottom of stem wire to secure wire in place.

Hide yarn tails inside Candy Cane.

Bend rod into a candy cane shape: bending around a spool of thread or a small bottle will help get a nice curve.

Attach jump ring (see page 80).

Mistletoe Truffle

SUPPLIES

G6/4mm crochet hook

Worsted weight yarn in brown, white, red and green

Glue (see page 8)

Polyester fiberfill stuffing

Jump ring, 10mm

TRUFFLE

With brown yarn, make a magic ring, ch 1.

Rnd 1: 6 sc in ring, pull ring closed tight (6 sts).

Rnd 2: 2 sc in each st around. Place marker for beginning of rnd and move marker up as each rnd is completed (12 sts).

Rnd 3: *sc in next st, 2 sc in next st* 6 times (18 sts).

Rnd 4: *sc in next 2 sts, 2 sc in next st* 6 times (24 sts).

Rnd 5: *sc in next 3 sts, 2 sc in next st* 6 times (30 sts).

Rnd 6: *sc in next 4 sts, 2 sc in next st* 6 times (36 sts).

Rnds 7-13: sc in each st around.

Rnd 14: *sc in next 4 sts, invdec* 6 times (30 sts).

Rnd 15: *sc in next 3 sts, invdec* 6 times (24 sts).

Start to stuff and continue stuffing after each rnd.

Rnd 16: *sc in next 2 sts, invdec* 6 times (18 sts).

Rnd 17: *sc in next st, invdec* 6 times (12 sts).

Rnd 18: invdec 6 times (6 sts).

Fasten off. Finish adding stuffing.

To close hole, thread tail in yarn needle, insert needle thru front loop of each st around opening and pull tight. Weave in end. Squeeze ball into a nice round shape.

FROSTING

With white yarn, make a magic ring, ch 1.

Rnd 1: 6 sc in ring, pull ring closed tight (6 sts).

Rnd 2: 2 sc in each st around. Place marker for beginning of rnd and move marker up as each rnd is completed (12 sts).

Rnd 3: *sc in next st, 2 sc in next st* 6 times (18 sts).

Rnd 4: *sc in next 2 sts, 2 sc in next st* 6 times (24 sts).

Rnd 5: *sc in next 3 sts, 2 sc in next st* 6 times (30 sts).

Rnd 6: *sc in next 4 sts, 2 sc in next st* 6 times (36 sts).

Rnd 7: *sc in next 8 sts, 2 sc in next st* 4 times (40 sts).

Rnd 8: *sl st in next st, sc in next st, hdc in next st, dc in next st, 3 tr in next st, dc in next st, hdc in next st, sc in next st* 5 times. Fasten off.

LEAVES

The leaves are made with green yarn in 5 connected rows.

Leaf 1: ch 9, dc in 2nd ch from hook, dc in next 4 ch, sl st in next 3 ch (8 sts).

Leaves 2-5: repeat Leaf 1. Fasten off. Knot tails together.

BERRIES (MAKE 3)

With red yarn, make a magic ring, ch 1.

Rnd 1: 5 hdc in ring, pull ring closed tight, join with sl st in first st. Fasten off.

Push on center of Rnd 1 to pop Berry into shape, knot tails together and roll Berry between fingers to make it round.

FINISHING

Glue Frosting to top of Truffle.

Sew tails of Leaves into center-top of Truffle to hide them inside. Glue Leaves to Frosting as shown in picture—holding them in place with pins until glue dries. Sew Berries on Leaves.

Attach jump ring (see page 80).

Snow Cone

SUPPLIES

G6/4mm crochet hook

Worsted weight yarn in pink, yellow, green, blue and white

Polyester fiberfill stuffing

Jump ring, 10mm

ICE BALL

With pink yarn, make a magic ring, ch 1.

Rnd 1: 6 sc in ring, pull ring closed tight (6 sts).

Rnd 2: 2 sc in each st around. Place marker for beginning of rnd and move marker up as each rnd is completed (12 sts).

Rnd 3: *sc in next st, 2 sc in next st* 6 times (18 sts).

Rnd 4: *sc in next 2 sts, 2 sc in next st* 6 times (24 sts).

Rnd 5: *sc in next 3 sts, 2 sc in next st* 6 times; change to yellow yarn in last st (30 sts).

Rnd 6: *sc in next 4 sts, 2 sc in next st* 6 times (36 sts).

Rnds 7-9: sc in each st around; change to green yarn in last st.

Rnds 10-13: sc in each st around; change to blue yarn in last st.

Rnd 14: *sc in next 4 sts, invdec* 6 times (30 sts).

Rnd 15: *sc in next 3 sts, invdec* 6 times (24 sts).

Start to stuff and continue stuffing after each rnd.

Rnd 16: *sc in next 2 sts, invdec* 6 times (18 sts).

Rnd 17: *sc in next st, invdec* 6 times (12 sts).

Rnd 18: invdec 6 times (6 sts).

Fasten off. Finish adding stuffing.

To close hole, thread tail in yarn needle, insert needle thru front loop of each st around opening and pull tight. Weave in end.

Squeeze ball into a nice round shape.

CONE

With white yarn, make a magic ring, ch 1.

Rnd 1: 6 sc in ring, pull ring closed tight (6 sts).

Rnd 2: *sc in next st, 2 sc in next st* 3 times. Place marker for beginning of rnd and move marker up as each rnd is completed (9 sts).

Rnd 3: *sc in next 2 sts, 2 sc in next st* 3 times (12 sts).

Rnd 4: sc in each st around.

Rnd 5: *sc in next st, 2 sc in next st* 6 times (18 sts).

Rnd 6: sc in each st around.

Rnd 7: *2 sc in next st, sc in next 2 sts* 6 times (24 sts).

Rnd 8: sc in each st around.

Rnd 9: *sc in next 3 sts, 2 sc in next st* 6 times (30 sts).

Rnd 10: sc in each st around.

Rnd 11: *2 sc in next st, sc in next 4 sts* 6 times (36 sts).

Rnd 12: sc in each st around.

Rnd 13: *sc in next 5 sts, 2 sc in next st* 6 times (42 sts).

Rnd 14: sc in each st around.

Rnd 15: *2 sc in next st, sc in next 6 sts* 6 times (48 sts).

Rnd 16: sc in each st around.

Rnd 17: sl st in each st around.

Fasten off.

FINISHING

Stuff lower half of Cone. Place Ice Ball in Cone so that color-change jogs on Ice Ball face down and Rnds 1 and 18 of Ice Ball meet edge of Cone. Sew in place. Weave in end.

Squeeze Cone into shape.

Attach jump ring (see page 80).

Snowflake Macaron

Have fun making these cookies in lots of bright colors!

SUPPLIES

G6/4mm crochet hook

Worsted weight yarn in blue and white

Polyester fiberfill stuffing

Jump ring, 10mm

★ INVISIBLE FINISH USED IN THIS PATTERN

This technique is also called an Invisible Join.

1. Work rnd according to pattern.

2. While hook remains in st, cut off yarn with a 4" tail and pull tail right thru the st (do not yarn over).

3. Thread tail in yarn needle.

4. Sew under both loops of **first st** of rnd.

5. Sew down into center "V" of **last st** worked in rnd.

6. Tighten gently until loop looks like other sts of rnd. Weave in end.

COOKIE (MAKE 2)

With blue yarn, make a magic ring, ch 1.

Rnd 1: 6 sc in ring, pull ring closed tight (6 sts).

Rnd 2: 2 sc in each st around. Place marker for beginning of rnd and move marker up as each rnd is completed (12 sts).

Rnd 3: *sc in next st, 2 sc in next st* 6 times (18 sts).

Rnd 4: *sc in next 2 sts, 2 sc in next st* 6 times (24 sts).

Rnd 5: *sc in next st, 2 sc in next st, sc in next 2 sts* 6 times (30 sts).

Rnd 6: *sc in next 3 sts, 2 sc in next st, sc in next st* 6 times (36 sts).

Rnd 7: *sc in next 5 sts, 2 sc in next st* 6 times; change to white yarn in last st (42 sts).

Be careful not to make your sl sts too tight in the next rnd. You will work into them to connect the Cookie halves.

Rnd 8: working in **back loops only**, sl st in each st around until 1 st remains, join to first st with invisible finish (see ★). Weave in ends.

FINISHING

To connect Cookie halves, place them wrong sides together so that white rnds touch. Using white yarn, work stitch by stitch thru both layers with sl st in **outer loops only** by inserting your hook in the white loops that adjoin blue on each piece. Pause to stuff when pieces are nearly connected. Fasten off. Weave in end.

Squeeze into a disc shape.

Mark end points for spokes of snowflake by placing 6 pins in groove between Rnds 6-7. With white yarn, embroider snowflake as shown in picture.

Attach jump ring (see page 80).

Ribbon Candy

The Ribbon Candy is made from a striped strip that is folded into loops.

SUPPLIES

G6/4mm crochet hook

Worsted weight yarn in pink, white & green

Skewer or knitting needle

Jump ring, 10mm

Note: A chain 1 at the beginning of a row is for turning your work and does not count as a stitch.

With green yarn, ch 86.

Row 1: sc in 2nd ch from hook and in each remaining ch across (85 sts).

Row 2: ch 1, turn, sl st in each st across. Fasten off.

The next row is made along remaining unworked edge of starting chain.

Row 3: turn, join white yarn in first ch with sl st, ch 2 (counts as first hdc), hdc in each remaining ch across (85 sts). Fasten off.

Row 4: turn, join pink yarn in first hdc with sl st, ch 1 (counts as first sc), sc in each remaining st across (85 sts).

Row 5: ch 1, turn, sc in each st across. Fasten off.

Row 6: turn, join white yarn in first sc with sl st, ch 2 (counts as first hdc), hdc in each remaining st across (85 sts). Fasten off.

Row 7: turn, join green yarn in first hdc with sl st, ch 1 (counts as first sc), sc in each remaining st across (85 sts).

Row 8: ch 1, turn, sl st in each st across. Fasten off.

Weave in ends.

FINISHING

Shape strip into loops as shown in picture and hold in place with a skewer or knitting needle.

Using pink yarn, connect touching edges (see 4 dots above) with a stitch thru pink stripe. Remove skewer.

Attach jump ring (see page 80) over the st you sewed at Dot 1.

STARLIGHT PEPPERMINT

The Peppermint is an intermediate-level pattern due to all of the color changes.

• To change color, work last stitch of old color to last yarn over, yarn over with new color and pull thru both loops to complete the stitch.

• Carry unused color across top of previous row and crochet over it to encase the strand.

• Pull gently on the strand you are carrying after each color change to remove excess slack.

When doing color work such as this, the yarn tends to tangle. Check your working yarn at the end of each rnd and untwist as needed; or, to prevent tangles, keep one color to the front and one color to the back. For a video demo of this technique, visit my Amigurumi Tutorials board on Pinterest (see page 81).

SUPPLIES

G6/4mm crochet hook

Worsted weight yarn in red and white

Polyester fiberfill stuffing

Jump ring, 10mm

With **white** yarn, make a magic ring, ch 1.

Rnd 1: 7 sc in ring, pull ring closed tight (7 sts).

Get ready to introduce red yarn in the next rnd: use it for the yarn over of your first st.

Rnd 2: *sc in next st **w/white**, sc in same st **w/red*** 7 times; change to **white** yarn in last st (14 sts). Place marker for beginning of rnd and move marker up as each rnd is completed.

Rnd 3: *2 sc in next st **w/white**, sc in next st **w/red*** 7 times; change to **white** yarn in last st (21 sts).

Rnd 4: *sc in next 2 sts **w/white**, 2 sc in next st **w/red*** 7 times; change to **white** yarn in last st (28 sts).

Rnd 5: *2 sc in next st **w/white**, sc in next st **w/white**, sc in next 2 sts **w/red*** 7 times; change to **white** yarn in last st (35 sts).

Rnd 6: *sc in next 3 sts **w/white**, sc in next st **w/red**, 2 sc in next st **w/red*** 7 times; change to **white** yarn in last st (42 sts).

Rnds 7-10: *sc in next 3 sts **w/white**, sc in next 3 sts **w/red*** 7 times; change to **white** yarn in last st (42 sts).

Knot starting tails together.

Rnd 11: *sc in next 3 sts **w/white**, sc in next st **w/red**, sc2tog **w/red*** 7 times; change to **white** yarn in last st (35 sts).

Rnd 12: *sc2tog **w/white**, sc in next st **w/white**, sc in next 2 sts **w/red*** 7 times; change to **white** yarn in last st (28 sts).

Rnd 13: *sc in next 2 sts **w/white**, sc2tog **w/red*** 7 times; change to **white** yarn in last st (21 sts).

Start to stuff and continue stuffing after each rnd.

Rnd 14: *sc2tog **w/white**, sc in next st **w/red*** 7 times; change to **white** yarn in last st (14 sts).

Cut off **red** yarn with 4" tail.

Rnd 15: *sc2tog **w/white*** 7 times (7 sts).

Sl st in next st. Fasten off. Finish adding stuffing.

To close hole, thread tail in yarn needle, insert needle thru front loop of each st around opening and pull tight. Weave in end. Squeeze into disc shape.

FINISHING

Attach jump ring (see page 80).

Taffy Twirl

SUPPLIES

G6/4mm crochet hook

Worsted weight yarn in pink and yellow

Polyester fiberfill stuffing

Jump ring, 10mm

Note: A ch 1 at the beginning of a row is for turning your work and does not count as a st.

TAFFY

With pink yarn, ch 21.

Row 1: 2 sc in 2nd ch from hook, sc in next 17 chs, sc2tog. Place marker for beginning of row and move marker up as each row is completed (20 sts).

Work in **back loops only** for **Rows 2-12**.

Row 2: ch 1, turn, sc2tog, sc in next 17 sts, 2 sc in next st; change to yellow yarn in last st (20 sts).

Row 3: ch 1, turn, 2 sc in next st, sc in next 17 sts, sc2tog (20 sts).

Row 4: ch 1, turn, sc2tog, sc in next 17 sts, 2 sc in next st; change to pink yarn in last st (20 sts).

Row 5: ch 1, turn, 2 sc in next st, sc in next 17 sts, sc2tog (20 sts).

Row 6: ch 1, turn, sc2tog, sc in next 17 sts, 2 sc in next st; change to yellow yarn in last st (20 sts).

Row 7: ch 1, turn, 2 sc in next st, sc in next 17 sts, sc2tog (20 sts).

Row 8: ch 1, turn, sc2tog, sc in next 17 sts, 2 sc in next st; change to pink yarn in last st (20 sts).

Row 9: ch 1, turn, 2 sc in next st, sc in next 17 sts, sc2tog (20 sts).

Row 10: ch 1, turn, sc2tog, sc in next 17 sts, 2 sc in next st; change to yellow yarn in last st (20 sts).

Row 11: ch 1, turn, 2 sc in next st, sc in next 17 sts, sc2tog (20 sts).

Row 12: ch 1, turn, sc2tog, sc in next 17 sts, 2 sc in next st (20 sts).

Row 13: ch 1, turn, fold work right sides together so that Corner A meets Corner B.

Sl st thru both layers to connect Rows 1 and 12: Work stitch-by-stitch going thru **both loops** of Row 12 and the chs of Row 1. The fabric will twist as you go and feel a bit awkward. This creates the spiral formation of the stripes.

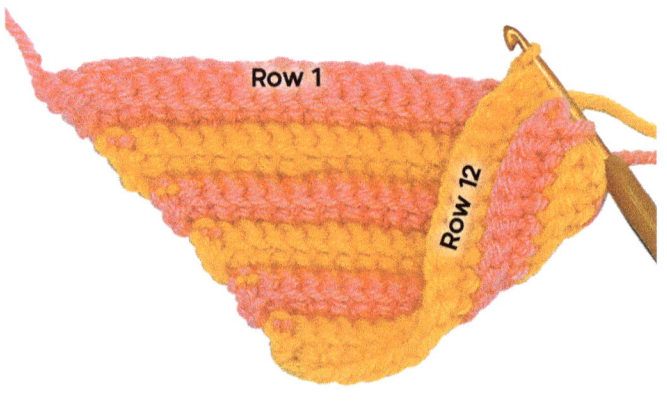

Fasten off. Weave tail thru sts at end, pull tight to close hole and secure with a knot.

Turn Taffy right-side out and stuff. Sew 2nd end closed same as 1st end.

Squeeze into a cylinder.

WRAPPER (MAKE 2)

With pink yarn, make a magic ring, ch 1.

Rnd 1: 10 sc in ring, pull ring closed tight (10 sts).

Rnd 2: working in **back loops only**, *dc in next st, 2 dc in next st* 5 times (15 sts).

Rnd 3: resuming work in **both loops**, 2 dc in each st around (30 sts).

Sl st in next st. Fasten off.

FINISHING

Sew a Wrapper to each end of Taffy with right sides together. Pinch Wrapper into a ruffled shape as shown in picture.

Attach jump ring (see page 80) to edge of Wrapper.

PINWHEEL POP

SUPPLIES

G6/4mm crochet hook

Jump ring, 10mm

Glue (optional, see page 8)

Worsted weight yarn in aqua and purple

6" lollipop stick, skewer or dowel

OUTER STRIPE

With aqua yarn, loosely ch 72.

Row 1: dc in 3rd ch from hook and in each remaining ch across (70 sts). Fasten off.

INNER STRIPE

With purple yarn, loosely ch 52.

Row 1: dc in 3rd ch from hook and in each remaining ch across (50 sts). Fasten off.

FINISHING

Lay inner stripe on top of outer stripe offset 1/2" from end. Roll stripes into a coil as shown in picture. Secure ends with sts then sew yarn tails back and forth thru diameter several times to hold the shape.

Push, twist and wiggle stick thru diameter of circle, going into gaps between stitches. Stop just before piercing opposite edge.

If further reinforcement is desired, insert tip of glue bottle randomly between coils and apply glue. Place some glue where yarn strips meet stick to secure stick.

Attach jump ring (see page 80).

CUT-OUT COOKIES

Cut-Out Cookies are made in 2 pieces: a Frosting layer and a Cookie layer. A stiff type of yarn is best—and the same brand and type should be used for both layers. Otherwise, it can be tricky to get the pieces properly sized so that the Cookie peeks past the Frosting. In that case, experiment with different sizes of hooks until you get the right fit.

The Frosting layer is stiffened with a mixture of glue and water. If you've never done this, get ready for some fun! The results are very exciting. It's easy—and ideal for this pattern. Bugle bead 'sprinkles' are the perfect finishing touch.

SUPPLIES

G6/4mm crochet hook

Worsted weight yarn in red, green, yellow, turquoise, white, pink, brown and beige

Bugle beads in assorted colors, 6mm

Glue (see page 8)

Foil or wax paper

Small paint brush

Small bowl

Bent nose tweezers

Jump rings, 10mm

Note: A chain 1 or 2 at the beginning of a row is for turning your work and does not count as a stitch.

★ HOW TO STIFFEN CROCHETED FABRIC

Your favorite brand of white glue will work fine.

1. In a small dish, stir together a mixture of approximately 60% glue and 40% water. The mixture is very forgiving, so don't worry about measuring.

2. Place piece wrong-side up on foil or wax paper. (Glue is only applied to the wrong side so that the right side retains the pretty finish of the yarn.)

3. Paint glue mixture on surface until it is well covered.

4. Let dry. Be patient—it can take several days for the glue to completely dry.

Repeat if more stiffness is desired.

FINISHING

These Finishing instructions are used for all Cut-Out Cookies.

Stiffen wrong side of Frosting (see instructions above).

Glue Frosting to Cookie with wrong sides together.

Glue bugle beads to Frosting: Bent nose tweezers are especially helpful for this. Squeeze some glue on a scrap of foil or paper. Grip bead with tweezers, dip lightly in glue, drop in place on ornament and tap with your finger to press bead into the fabric.

Attach jump ring (see page 80).

BELL

FROSTING

With yellow yarn, loosely ch 4.

Row 1: sc in 2nd ch from hook and in each remaining st across (3 sts).

Row 2: ch 1, turn, 2 sc in first st, sc in next st, 2 sc in last st (5 sts).

Row 3: ch 1, turn, 2 sc in first st, sc in next 3 sts, 2 sc in last st (7 sts).

Rows 4-5: ch 1, turn, sc in each st across.

Row 6: ch 1, turn, 2 sc in first st, sc in next 5 sts, 2 sc in last st (9 sts).

Rows 7-8: ch 1, turn, sc in each st across.

Row 9: ch 1, turn, 2 sc in first st, sc in next 7 sts, 2 sc in last st (11 sts).

Rows 10-13: ch 1, turn, sc in each st across.

Row 14: ch 1, turn, 2 sc in first st, sc in next 9 sts, 2 sc in last st (13 sts).

Row 15: ch 1, turn, sc in next 6 sts, (hdc, 3 dc, hdc) in next st, sc in next 6 sts (12 sts + 1 scallop).

Rnd 16: sl st around perimeter.

Fasten off. Weave in ends.

COOKIE

With beige yarn, loosely ch 4.

Rows 1-15: make the same as Frosting.

Rnd 16: hdc around perimeter making 3 sts in same st at lower corners.

Join with sl st in first st. Fasten off. Weave in ends.

FINISHING

See page 50.

ANGEL

FROSTING

For **head**, using white yarn, make a magic ring, ch 1.

Rnd 1: 5 sc in ring, pull ring closed tight (5 sts).

Rnd 2: 2 sc in each st around. Place marker for beginning of rnd and move marker up as each rnd is completed (10 sts).

Rnd 3: *sc in next st, 2 sc in next* 5 times (15 sts).

Now work in rows to make **wings**.

Row 4: ch 1, turn, 2 sc in next 5 sts around head (10 sts).

Row 5: ch 1, turn, sc in each st across.

Row 6: ch 1, turn, 2 sc in each st across (20 sts).

Row 7: ch 1, turn, sc in each st across.

Fasten off.

Hold work right side up with head pointed down.

Row 8: for **dress**, join with sc in 8th st, sc in same st, 2 sc in next 5 sts (12 sts).

Row 9: ch 1, turn, sc in each st across.

Row 10: ch 1, turn, 2 sc in first st, sc in next 10 sts, 2 sc in last st (14 sts).

Row 11: ch 1, turn, sc in each st across.

Row 12: ch 1, turn, 2 sc in first st, sc in next 12 sts, 2 sc in last st (16 sts).

Row 13: ch 1, turn, sc in each st across.

Row 14: ch 1, turn, 2 sc in first st, sc in next 14 sts, 2 sc in last st (18 sts).

Row 15: ch 1, turn, sc in each st across.

Row 16: for **scallops**, ch 1, turn, *skip next 2 sts, 5 dc in next st, skip next 2 sts, sl st in next st* 3 times.

Fasten off. Weave in ends.

COOKIE

For **head**, using beige yarn, make a magic ring, ch 1.

Rnds/Rows 1-16: make the same as Frosting.

Rnd 17: hdc around perimeter making 3 sts in same st at corners **except** sl st instead of hdc at base of head, wings, and center scallop (see red dots below).

Join with sl st in first st. Fasten off. Weave in ends.

FINISHING

See page 50.

GINGERBREAD MAN

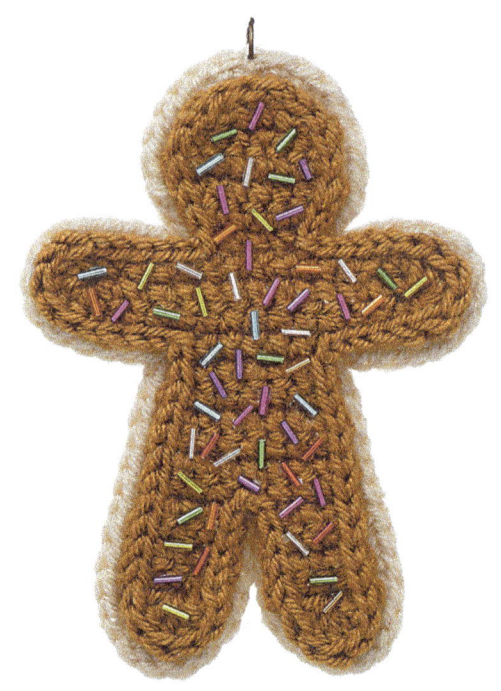

FROSTING

For **arms**, with brown yarn, loosely ch 15.

Row 1: sc in 2nd ch from hook and in each remaining ch across (14 sts).

Rows 2-3: ch 1, turn, sc in each st across.

Fasten off.

Row 4: for **body**, turn, join with sc in 5th st, sc in next 5 sts (6 sts).

Row 5: ch 1, turn sc in each st across.

Row 6: ch 1, turn, 2 sc in first st, sc in next 4 sts, 2 sc in last st (8 sts).

Rows 7-9: ch 1, turn, sc in each st across.

Row 10: for **1st leg**, ch 1, turn, sc in next 4 sts (4 sts).

Rows 11-14: ch 1, turn, sc in each st across.

Fasten off.

Row 15: for **2nd leg**, join with sc in Row 9 beside 1st leg, sc in each remaining st across (4 sts).

Rows 16-19: ch 1, turn, sc in each st across.

Fasten off.

Hold work right side up with legs pointed down.

Row 20: for **head**, join with sc in 6th st of arm, sc in next 3 sts (4 sts).

Row 21: ch 1, turn, 2 sc in 1st st, sc in next 2 sts, 2 sc in last st (6 sts).

Row 22: ch 1, turn, 2 sc in 1st st, sc in next 4 sts, 2 sc in last st (8 sts).

Row 23: ch 1, turn, sc in each st across.

Row 24: ch 1, turn, sc2tog, sc in next 4 sts, sc2tog (6 sts).

Row 25: ch 1, turn, sc2tog, sc in next 2 sts, sc2tog (4 sts).

Row 26: ch 1, turn, sc in 1st st, sc2tog, sc in last st (3 sts).

Rnd 27: sl st around perimeter **except** at ends of arms and legs, 5 dc in center st instead of sl st. This makes a scallop to create rounded hands and feet.

Fasten off. Weave in ends.

COOKIE

Using beige yarn, loosely ch 15.

Rows 1-26: make the same as Frosting.

Rnd 27: ch 1, hdc around perimeter **except** at ends of arms and legs, 5 dc in center st instead of hdc and sl st instead of hdc at neck, armpits and crotch.

Join with sl st in first st. Fasten off. Weave in ends.

FINISHING

See page 50.

TREE

FROSTING

With green yarn, loosely ch 14.

Row 1: sc in 2nd ch from hook and in each remaining ch across (13 sts).

Row 2: ch 1, turn, sc2tog, sc in next 9 sts, sc2tog (11 sts).

Row 3: ch 1, turn, sc in each st across.

Row 4: ch 1, turn, sc2tog, sc in next 7 sts, sc2tog (9 sts).

Row 5: ch 1, turn, sc in each st across.

Row 6: ch 1, turn, sc2tog, sc in next 5 sts, sc2tog (7 sts).

Rows 7-8: ch 1, turn, sc in each st across.

Row 9: ch 1, turn, sc2tog, sc in next 3 sts, sc2tog (5 sts).

Row 10: ch 1, turn, sc in each st across.

Row 11: ch 1, turn, sc2tog, sc in next st, sc2tog (3 sts).

Row 12: ch 1, turn, sc in each st across.

In next row, **sc3tog** as follows: insert hook in st, yo, pull up a loop (2 loops on hook). Repeat 2 more times (4 loops on hook). Yo, pull thru all 4 loops on hook.

Row 13: ch 1, turn, **sc3tog** (1 st).

Fasten off.

Hold work right side up with top of Tree pointed down.

Row 14: for **trunk,** join with sc in 6th st, sc in next 2 sts (3 sts).

Rows 15-16: ch 1, turn, sc in each st across.

Rnd 17: sl st around perimeter.

Fasten off. Weave in ends.

COOKIE

With beige yarn, loosely ch 14.

Rows 1-16: make the same as Frosting.

Rnd 17: hdc around perimeter making 3 sts in same st at corners **except** sl st instead of hdc where trunk joins tree.

Join with sl st in first st. Fasten off. Weave in ends.

FINISHING

See page 50.

CANDY CANE

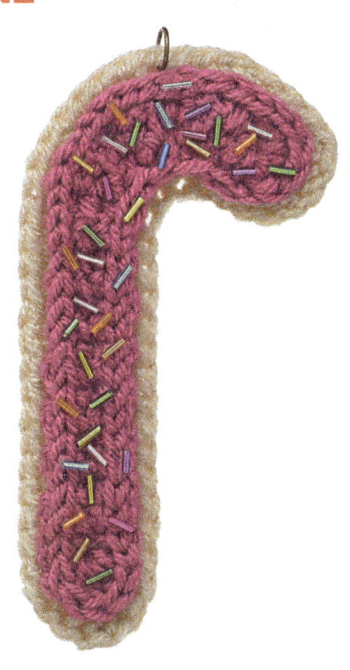

FROSTING

With red yarn, loosely ch 4.

Row 1: sc in 2nd ch from hook and in each remaining ch across (3 sts).

Rows 2-14: ch 1, turn, sc in each st across.

Row 15: ch 1, turn, sc in first st, hdc in next st, dc in last st (3 sts).

Row 16: ch 2, turn, dc in first st, hdc in next st, sc in last st (3 sts).

Row 17: ch 1, turn, sc in first st, hdc in next st, dc in last st (3 sts).

Row 18: ch 2, turn, dc in first st, hdc in next st, sc in last st (3 sts).

Row 19: ch 1, turn, sc in first st, hdc in next st, dc in last st (3 sts).

Row 20: ch 2, turn, dc in first st, hdc in next st, sc in last st (3 sts).

Row 21: ch 1, turn, sc in first st, hdc in next st, dc in last st (3 sts).

Row 22: ch 2, turn, dc in first st, hdc in next st, sc in last st (3 sts).

Note: In next rnd, **slst2tog** as follows: insert hook in st, yo and pull up a loop, insert hook in next st, yo and pull thru all loops on hook.

Rnd 23: turn work so that curve of cane faces right (⌐). Sl st around perimeter **except** 5 dc in center st at each end (scallop) instead of sl st *and* **slst2tog** around inside curve to emphasize the shape.

Sl st in next st. Fasten off. Weave in ends.

COOKIE

With beige yarn, loosely ch 4.

Rows 1-22: make the same as Frosting.

Note: In next rnd, **hdc2tog** as follows: yo, insert hook in st, pull up a loop (3 loops on hook), yo, insert hook in next st, pull up a loop (5 loops on hook), yo, pull thru all 5 loops on hook.

Rnd 23: ch 1, with curve of cane facing left (⌐), hdc around perimeter **except hdc2tog** around inside curve to emphasize the shape *and* 5 dc in center st at each end instead of hdc (scallop).

Join with sl st in first st. Fasten off. Weave in ends.

FINISHING

See page 50.

STAR

FROSTING

With turquoise yarn, make a magic ring, ch 1.

Rnd 1: 5 sc in ring, pull ring closed tight (5 sts).

Rnd 2: 2 sc in each st around. Place marker for beginning of rnd and move marker up as each rnd is completed (10 sts).

Rnd 3: *sc in next st, 2 sc in next st* 5 times (15 sts).

Rnd 4: *sc in next 2 sts, 2 sc in next st* 5 times (20 sts).

Rnd 5: *sc in next 3 sts, 2 sc in next st* 5 times (25 sts).

Now work in rows.

POINT 1

Row 1: sc in next 5 sts (5 sts).

Row 2: ch 1, turn, sc2tog, sc next 3 sts (4 sts).

Row 3: ch 1, turn, sc2tog, sc next 2 sts (3 sts).

Row 4: ch 1, turn, sc2tog, sc in next st (2 sts).

Row 5: ch 1, turn, sc2tog (1 st).

Fasten off.

POINTS 2-5

Join with sc in Rnd 5 beside Point just made.

Row 1: sc in next 4 sts (5 sts).

Rows 2-5: make the same as Point 1.

Now work a rnd.

Rnd 6: sl st around perimeter; at tip of each point (sl st, ch 1, sl st).

Fasten off. Weave in ends.

COOKIE

With beige yarn, make a magic ring, ch 1.

Rnds 1-5: make the same as Frosting.

Points: make the same as Frosting thru Point 5, Row 5.

Rnd 6: hdc around perimeter **except** sl st instead of hdc at base of each point *and* (hdc, ch 2, hdc) at tip of each point.

Join with sl st in first st. Fasten off. Weave in ends.

FINISHING

See page 50.

HEART

The Heart is made around a foundation chain as one continuous round.

FROSTING

With pink yarn, loosely ch 15.

Rnd 1: 3 sc in 2nd ch from hook, sc in next 5 chs, skip 2 chs, sc in next 5 chs, 3 sc in last ch …

(Half of Rnd 1 is now done. Work next sts around other side of chain.)

… turn, sc in next 5 chs, (sc, ch 2, sc) in ch-2 space, sc in next 5 chs. Place marker for beginning of rnd and move marker up as each rnd is completed (28 sts + 2 chs).

Rnd 2: 2 sc in first 3 sts, sc in next 4 sts, skip 2 sts, sc in next 4 sts, 2 sc in next 3 sts …

continue around bottom of Heart

… sc in next 6 sts, (sc, ch 2, sc) in ch-2 space, sc in last 6 sts (34 sts + 2 chs).

Rnd 3: 2 sc in next 6 sts, sc in next 3 sts, skip 2 sts, sc in next 3 sts, 2 sc in next 6 sts …

continue around bottom of Heart

… sc in next 7 sts, (sc, ch 2, sc) in ch-2 space, sc in next 7 sts (46 sts + 2 chs).

Rnd 4: sc in next 6 sts, 2 sc in next 2 sts, sc in next 6 sts, skip 2 sts, sc in next 6 sts, 2 sc in next 2 sts …

continue around bottom of Heart

… sc in next 14 sts, (sc, ch 2, sc) in ch-2 space, sc in next 9 sts (51 sts + 2 chs).

Join with invisible finish in first st (see page 45). Fasten off. Weave in ends.

COOKIE

With beige yarn, loosely ch 15.

Rnds 1-3: make the same as Frosting.

Rnd 4: ch 1, hdc in next 6 sts, 2 hdc in next 2 sts, hdc in next 6 sts, skip 2 sts, hdc in next 6 sts, 2 hdc in next 2 sts …

continue around bottom of Heart

… hdc in next 14 sts, (hdc, ch 2, hdc) in ch-2 space, hdc in next 9 sts (51 sts + 2 chs).

Join with invisible finish in first st (see page 45). Fasten off. Weave in ends.

Note: If there are visible holes in your foundation chain, weave tails thru sts to fill in the gaps.

FINISHING

See page 50.

Animal Friends

Snowy Owl

This pattern is created with 3 yarn weights. The 2-tone area of Head is made by working with 2 strands of yarn held together. If you've never crocheted with multiple strands, just pretend you are working with a single strand and make each st as if you were holding 1 strand of yarn.

SUPPLIES

G6/4mm crochet hook
Super Fine yarn in black
DK, Light Worsted yarn in white and black
Worsted weight yarn in white
2 yellow animal eyes, 12mm
Glue (see page 8)
Polyester fiberfill stuffing
Jump ring, 10mm

HEAD

With Worsted weight yarn in white, make a magic ring, ch 1.

Rnd 1: 6 sc in ring, pull ring closed tight (6 sts).

Rnd 2: 2 sc in each st around. Place marker for beginning of rnd and move marker up as each rnd is completed (12 sts).

Rnd 3: *sc in next st, 2 sc in next st* 6 times (18 sts).

Rnd 4: *sc in next 2 sts, 2 sc in next st* 6 times (24 sts).

Rnd 5: *sc in next 3 sts, 2 sc in next st* 6 times (30 sts).

At the end of the next rnd, you will change from a single strand of Worsted weight yarn to 2 strands of designated yarn held together.

Rnd 6: *sc in next 4 sts, 2 sc in next st* 6 times; change in last st to DK, Light Worsted yarn in white and Super Fine yarn in black (36 sts).

Now work with 2 strands of yarn held together.

Rnds 7-13: sc in each st around.

Rnd 14: *sc in next 4 sts, sc2tog* 6 times (30 sts).

Rnd 15: *sc in next 3 sts, sc2tog* 6 times (24 sts).

Start to stuff and continue stuffing after each rnd.

Rnd 16: *sc in next 2 sts, sc2tog* 6 times (18 sts).

Rnd 17: *sc in next st, sc2tog* 6 times (12 sts).

Rnd 18: sc2tog 6 times (6 sts).

Fasten off. Finish adding stuffing.

To close hole, thread tail in yarn needle, insert needle thru front loop of each st around opening and pull tight. Weave in end.

Squeeze Head into a nice round shape.

EYE RIMS (MAKE 2)

The Eye Rims are made using Loop Stitch (see page 77).

With Worsted weight yarn in white, make a magic ring, ch 1.

Rnd 1: 6 sc in ring, pull ring closed tight (6 sts).

Rnd 2: 2 lp st in each st around, join with sl st in next st (12 sts). Fasten off.

Sew ending tail down thru center "V" of next st. Trim yarn tails to length of loops. Pull on loops to set sts so they fan out like rays of the sun. Cut loops open and separate plies by running a blunt yarn needle thru strands. Trim fringe to about 1/2".

BEAK

With DK, Light Worsted yarn in black, ch 3.

Row 1: ch 1, turn, sc in each ch across (3 sts).

Fasten off.

FINISHING

Position tip of Beak at groove between Rnds 4-5, sew or glue in place and hide yarn tail inside Head.

Sew or glue Eye Rims to Head as shown in picture. Glue eyes to center of Eye Rims.

Attach jump ring (see page 80).

MOUSE

Twas the night before Christmas, and all through the house, not a creature was stirring ... not even this mouse!

SUPPLIES

G6/4mm crochet hook

Worsted weight yarn in gray, pink and white

2 black safety eyes, 8mm

Glue (see page 8)

Polyester fiberfill stuffing

Jump ring, 10mm

Note: A ch 1 at the beginning of a rnd is for turning your work and does not count as a st.

HEAD

With gray yarn, make a magic ring, ch 1.

Rnd 1: 6 sc in ring, pull ring closed tight (6 sts).

Rnd 2: *sc in next st, 2 sc in next st* 3 times. Place marker for beginning of rnd and move marker up as each rnd is completed (9 sts).

Rnd 3: *sc in next 2 sts, 2 sc in next st* 3 times (12 sts).

Rnd 4: *sc in next 2 sts, 2 sc in next st* 4 times (16 sts).

Rnd 5: *sc in next 3 sts, 2 sc in next st* 4 times (20 sts).

Rnd 6: *sc in next 4 sts, 2 sc in next st* 4 times (24 sts).

Rnd 7: *sc in next 5 sts, 2 sc in next st* 4 times (28 sts).

Rnd 8: *sc in next 6 sts, 2 sc in next st* 4 times (32 sts).

Rnd 9: *sc in next 7 sts, 2 sc in next st* 4 times (36 sts).

Rnds 10-16: sc in each st around.

Start to stuff and continue stuffing after each round.

Rnd 17: *sc in next 4 sts, invdec* 6 times (30 sts).

Rnd 18: *sc in next 3 sts, invdec* 6 times (24 sts).

Rnd 19: *sc in next 2 sts, invdec* 6 times (18 sts).

Rnd 20: *sc in next st, invdec* 6 times (12 sts).

Rnd 21: invdec 6 times (6 sts).

Fasten off. Finish adding stuffing.

To close hole, thread tail in yarn needle, insert needle thru front loop of each st around opening and pull tight. Weave in end. Squeeze Head into shape.

EARS (MAKE 2)

EAR FRONT

With pink yarn, make a magic ring, ch 1.

Rnd 1: 6 sc in ring, pull ring closed tight (6 sts).

Rnd 2: sc in next st, 2 dc in next 4 sts, sc in next st (10 sts).

Fasten off.

EAR BACK

With gray yarn, make a magic ring, ch 1.

Rnd 1: 6 sc in ring, pull ring closed tight (6 sts).

Rnd 2: sc in next st, 2 dc in next 4 sts, sc in next st (10 sts).

Rnd 3: ch 1, turn, place Ear Front against Ear Back with wrong sides facing and sts aligned. Working thru both layers, *sc in next st, 2 sc in next st* 5 times (15 sts).

Rnd 4: ch 1, turn, *sc in next 2 sts, 2 sc in next st* 5 times (20 sts).

Fasten off. Sew first 3 tails into space between layers of Ear to hide them, cut off excess.

FINISHING

Glue on eyes between Rnds 8-9 with an interspace of 6-7 sts.

Sew Ears with rims cupped on Rnd 14 of Head.

For **nose**, use pink yarn to embroider straight sts fanning out from center of Rnd 1 and extending out to Rnd 2.

For **whiskers**, use white yarn to embroider 3 long sts on each side of nose as shown in picture.

Attach jump ring (see page 80).

LION

Three rounds of loop stitch are used to create the Lion's mane. See page 77 if you're unfamiliar with this stitch. You may also want to visit YouTube to watch a video demo.

SUPPLIES

G6/4mm crochet hook

Worsted weight yarn in tan, white and black

2 black safety eyes, 8mm

Glue (see page 8)

Polyester fiberfill stuffing

Jump ring, 10mm

Note: A ch 1 at the beginning of a rnd or row is for turning your work and does not count as a st.

HEAD

With tan yarn, make a magic ring, ch 1.

Rnd 1: 6 sc in ring, pull ring closed tight (6 sts).

Rnd 2: *3 sc in next st, 2 sc in next st, sc in next st* twice. Place marker for beginning of rnd and move marker up as each rnd is completed (12 sts).

Rnd 3: sc in next st, 2 sc in next 3 sts, sc in next 3 sts, 2 sc in next 3 sts, sc in next 2 sts (18 sts).

Rnd 4: sc in next 2 sts, 2 sc in next st, *sc in next st, 2 sc in next st* twice, sc in next 4 sts, 2 sc in next st, *sc in next st, 2 sc in next st* twice, sc in next 2 sts (24 sts).

Rnd 5: sc in each st around (24 sts).

Rnd 6: *sc in next 3 sts, 2 sc in next st* 6 times (30 sts).

Rnd 7: sc in each st around.

Rnd 8: *sc in next 4 sts, 2 sc in next st* 6 times (36 sts).

Rnd 9: sc in each st around.

The work will change direction in Rnd 10 so that the loops for the Lion's mane are on the right side.

Rnd 10: ch 1, turn, lp st in each st around, join with sl st in first st (36 sts).

Rnds 11-12: ch 1, do not turn, lp st in each st around, join with sl st in first st (36 sts).

Rnd 13: ch 1, turn, sc in each st around, join with sl st in first st (36 sts).

Rnd 14: *sc in next 4 sts, invdec* 6 times (30 sts).

Rnd 15: *sc in next 3 sts, invdec* 6 times (24 sts).

Start to stuff and continue stuffing after each rnd.

Rnd 16: *sc in next 2 sts, invdec* 6 times (18 sts).

Rnd 17: *sc in next st, invdec* 6 times (12 sts).

Rnd 18: invdec 6 times (6 sts).

Fasten off. Finish adding stuffing.

To close hole, thread tail in yarn needle, insert needle thru front loop of each st around opening and pull tight. Weave in end.

Squeeze Head into an oval shape. Pull lp sts to set them in place to frame face as shown in picture.

NOSE

With tan yarn, ch 13.

Row 1: starting in 2nd ch from hook, sc in each st across (12 sts).

Rnd 2: ch 1, turn, working all the way around Row 1 and the starting chs, sc in each st around (24 sts).

Row 3: ch 1, do not turn, make 4 sts across end of strip, change to black yarn in last st (4 sts).

Row 4: ch 1, turn, sc in each st across (4 sts).

Row 5: ch 1, turn, sc2tog twice (2 sts).

Row 6: ch 1, turn, sc2tog (1 st).

Fasten off. Weave in ends except final black tail.

MUZZLE

With white yarn, make a magic ring, ch 1.

Rnd 1: 6 sc in ring, pull ring closed tight (6 sts).

Rnd 2: *3 sc in next st, 2 sc in next st, sc in next st* twice. Place marker for beginning of rnd and move marker up as each rnd is completed (12 sts).

Rnd 3: sc in next st, 2 sc in next 3 sts, sc in next 3 sts, 2 sc in next 3 sts, sc in next 2 sts (18 sts).

Fasten off. Weave in ends.

FINISHING

Assemble Nose and Muzzle as follows: Place Nose on Muzzle so that upper edge of black triangle meets edge of Muzzle (see A below). Pin in place. Thread black yarn tail onto needle, wrap tail to back of Muzzle (see B below), pull snugly and use tail to sew Nose to Muzzle by pushing needle up and down thru black area.

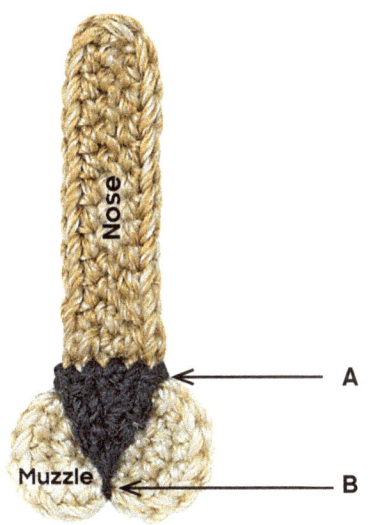

Glue Nose/Muzzle assembly to front of Head as shown in picture.

Glue on eyes as shown in picture.

Attach jump ring (see page 80).

SNOWSHOE HARE

SUPPLIES

G6/4mm crochet hook

Worsted weight yarn in white, pink and black

2 black safety eyes, 8mm

Glue (see page 8)

Polyester fiberfill stuffing

Jump ring, 10mm

Note: A chain 1 at the beginning of a rnd is for turning your work and does not count as a stitch.

HEAD

With white yarn, make a magic ring, ch 1.

Rnd 1: 6 sc in ring, pull ring closed tight (6 sts).

Rnd 2: 2 sc in each st around. Place marker for beginning of rnd and move marker up as each rnd is completed (12 sts).

Rnd 3: *sc in next 2 sts, 2 sc in next st* 4 times (16 sts).

Rnd 4: *sc in next 3 sts, 2 sc in next st* 4 times (20 sts).

Rnd 5: *sc in next 4 sts, 2 sc in next st* 4 times (24 sts).

Rnd 6: *sc in next 5 sts, 2 sc in next st* 4 times (28 sts).

Rnd 7: *sc in next 6 sts, 2 sc in next st* 4 times (32 sts).

Rnds 8-9: sc in each st around.

Rnd 10: *sc in next 7 sts, 2 sc in next st* 4 times (36 sts).

Rnds 11-14: sc in each st around.

Start to stuff and continue stuffing after each round.

Rnd 15: *sc in next 4 sts, invdec* 6 times (30 sts).

Rnd 16: *sc in next 3 sts, invdec* 6 times (24 sts).

Rnd 17: *sc in next 2 sts, invdec* 6 times (18 sts).

Rnd 18: *sc in next st, invdec* 6 times (12 sts).

Rnd 19: invdec 6 times (6 sts).

Fasten off. Finish adding stuffing.

To close hole, thread tail in yarn needle, insert needle thru front loop of each st around opening and pull tight. Weave in end. Squeeze Head into shape.

EARS (MAKE 2)

The ears are worked around a foundation chain.

EAR FRONT

With pink yarn, ch 10.

Rnd 1: starting in 2nd ch from hook, sc in next 8 chs, 3 sc in last ch, sc in next 8 ch (19 sts). Fasten off.

EAR BACK

With white yarn, ch 10.

Rnd 1: starting in 2nd ch from hook, sc in next 8 chs, 3 sc in last ch, sc in next 8 ch (19 sts).

Rnd 2: ch 1, turn, place Ear Front against Ear Back with wrong sides facing and sts aligned. Working thru both layers, sc in next 9 sts, 3 sc in next st, sc in next 9 sts (21 sts).

Rnd 3: ch 1, turn, sc in next 10 sts, 3 sc in next st, sc in next 10 sts (23 sts).

In the next rnd, you will change to black yarn for 9 sts to create the black ear tips. Carry the unused white yarn along top of previous row and crochet over it to encase the strand.

Rnd 4: ch 1, turn, sc in next 8 sts, change to black yarn in last st; sc in next 3 sts, 3 sc in next st, sc in next 3 sts, change to white yarn in last st; sc in next 8 sts (25 sts). Fasten off.

Sew first 3 tails into space between layers of Ear to hide them, cut off excess. Thread remaining tail in yarn needle, sew into opposite corner and pull tight. This will connect the corners and shape the Ear. Secure with a stitch and knot.

FINISHING

Glue on eyes between Rnds 7-8 with an interspace of 5-6 sts. Sew Ears on Rnds 11-13 of Head. For **nose**, embroider a "Y" with black yarn as shown in picture.

Attach jump ring (see page 80).

Fox

SUPPLIES

G6/4mm crochet hook

Worsted weight yarn in rust, white and black

2 gold or yellow slit-pupil safety eyes, 10mm

Black triangle animal nose, 10mm

Glue (see page 8)

Polyester fiberfill stuffing

Jump ring, 10mm

Note: A ch 1 at the beginning of a rnd or row is for turning your work and does not count as a st.

HEAD

With white yarn, make a magic ring, ch 1.

Rnd 1: 6 sc in ring, pull ring closed tight (6 sts).

Rnd 2: *sc in next st, 2 sc in next st* 3 times. Place marker for beginning of rnd and move marker up as each rnd is completed (9 sts).

Rnd 3: *sc in next 2 sts, 2 sc in next st* 3 times (12 sts).

Rnd 4: *sc in next 2 sts, 2 sc in next st* 4 times (16 sts).

Rnd 5: *sc in next 3 sts, 2 sc in next st* 4 times (20 sts).

Rnd 6: *sc in next 4 sts, 2 sc in next st* 4 times (24 sts).

Rnd 7: *sc in next 5 sts, 2 sc in next st* 4 times (28 sts).

Rnd 8: *sc in next 6 sts, 2 sc in next st* 4 times (32 sts).

Rnd 9: *sc in next 7 sts, 2 sc in next st* 4 times (36 sts).

Rnds 10-14: sc in each st around.

Start to stuff and continue stuffing after each round.

Rnd 15: *sc in next 4 sts, invdec* 6 times (30 sts).

Rnd 16: *sc in next 3 sts, invdec* 6 times (24 sts).

Rnd 17: *sc in next 2 sts, invdec* 6 times (18 sts).

Rnd 18: *sc in next st, invdec* 6 times (12 sts).

Rnd 19: invdec 6 times (6 sts).

Fasten off. Finish adding stuffing.

To close hole, thread tail in yarn needle, insert needle thru front loop of each st around opening and pull tight. Weave in end. Squeeze Head into shape.

HEAD CAP

With rust yarn, make a magic ring, ch 1.

Rnd 1: 6 sc in ring, pull ring closed tight (6 sts).

Rnd 2: 2 sc in each st around. Place marker for beginning of rnd and move marker up as each rnd is completed (12 sts).

Rnd 3: *sc in next st, 2 sc in next st* 6 times (18 sts).

Rnd 4: *sc in next 2 sts, 2 sc in next st* 6 times (24 sts).

Rnd 5: *sc in next 3 sts, 2 sc in next st* 6 times (30 sts).

Rnd 6: *sc in next 4 sts, 2 sc in next st* 6 times (36 sts).

Rnds 7-10: sc in each st around.

Now work in rows.

Row 11: sc in next 24 sts (24 sts).

Row 12: ch 1, turn, sc2tog, sc in next 20 sts, sc2tog (22 sts).

Row 13: ch 1, turn, sc2tog, sc in next 18 sts, sc2tog (20 sts).

Row 14: ch 1, turn, sc2tog, sc in next 16 sts, sc2tog (18 sts).

Row 15: ch 1, turn, sc2tog, sc in next 14 sts, sc2tog (16 sts).

Row 16: ch 1, turn, sc2tog, sc in next 12 sts, sc2tog (14 sts).

Row 17: ch 1, turn, sc2tog, sc in next 10 sts, sc2tog (12 sts).

Row 18: ch 1, turn, sc2tog, sc in next 8 sts, sc2tog (10 sts).

Row 19: ch 1, turn, sc2tog, sc in next 6 sts, sc2tog (8 sts).

Row 20: ch 1, turn, sc2tog, sc in next 4 sts, sc2tog (6 sts).

Row 21: ch 1, turn, sc2tog, sc in next 2 sts, sc2tog (4 sts).

Row 22: ch 1, turn, sc2tog twice (2 sts).

Row 23: ch 1, turn, sc2tog (1 st).

Rnd 24: ch 1, do not turn, sc around perimeter of entire piece. Fasten off.

EARS (MAKE 2)

The ears are worked around a foundation chain.

EAR FRONT

With white yarn, ch 5.

Rnd 1: starting in 2nd ch from hook, sc in next 3 chs, 3 sc in last ch, sc in next 3 ch (9 sts).

Rnd 2: ch 1, turn, sc in next 4 sts, 3 sc in next st, sc in next 4 sts (11 sts). Fasten off.

EAR BACK

With rust yarn, ch 5.

Rnd 1: starting in 2nd ch from hook, sc in next 3 chs, 3 sc in last ch, sc in next 3 ch (9 sts).

Rnd 2: ch 1, turn, sc in next 4 sts, 3 sc in next st, sc in next 4 sts (11 sts).

Rnd 3: ch 1, turn, place Ear Front against Ear Back with wrong sides facing and sts aligned. Working thru both layers, sc in next 5 sts, 3 sc in next st, sc in next 5 sts (13 sts).

Rnd 4: ch 1, turn, sc in next 6 sts, 3 sc in next st, sc in next 6 sts (15 sts). Fasten off.

Sew first 3 tails into space between layers of Ear to hide them, cut off excess. Thread remaining tail in yarn needle, sew into opposite corner and pull tight. This will connect the corners and shape the Ear. Secure with a stitch and knot.

Pinch tip of Ear into a point.

FINISHING

Sew or glue Head Cap on Head as shown in picture; sew yarn tail at tip of Cap into center front of Head.

Glue on eyes between Rnds 15-16 of Head Cap with an interspace of 7-8 sts.

Embroider **eye rims** with a double strand of black yarn.

Sew Ears on Rnds 7-9 of Head Cap.

Glue on nose as shown in picture.

Attach jump ring (see page 80).

Camel

An ornamental bridle makes the Camel very festive!

SUPPLIES

G6/4mm crochet hook

Worsted weight yarn in tan, black, red, purple, green and turquoise

2 black safety eyes, 8mm

2 gold buttons, 3/8"

Acrylic jewels in gold

Glue (see page 8)

Polyester fiberfill stuffing

Jump ring, 10mm

Note: A chain 1 at the beginning of a rnd or row is for turning your work and does not count as a stitch.

HEAD BACK

With tan yarn, make a magic ring, ch 1.

Rnd 1: 6 sc in ring, pull ring closed tight (6 sts).

Rnd 2: 2 sc in each st around. Place marker for beginning of rnd and move marker up as each rnd is completed (12 sts).

Rnd 3: *sc in next st, 2 sc in next st* 6 times (18 sts).

Rnd 4: *sc in next 2 sts, 2 sc in next st* 6 times (24 sts).

Rnd 5: *sc in next 3 sts, 2 sc in next st* 6 times (30 sts).

Rnd 6: *sc in next 4 sts, 2 sc in next st* 6 times (36 sts).

Rnds 7-12: sc in each st around.

Rnd 13: *sc in next 4 sts, invdec* 6 times (30 sts).

Rnd 14: *sc in next 3 sts, invdec* 6 times (24 sts).

Rnd 15: *sc in next 6 sts, invdec* 3 times (21 sts).

Rnd 16: sc in each st around. Fasten off.

HEAD FRONT (MAKE 2)

With tan yarn, ch 2.

Row 1: 3 sc in 2nd ch from hook (3 sts).

Row 2: ch 1, turn, 2 sc in each st across (6 sts).

Row 3: ch 1, turn, *sc in next st, 2 sc in next st* 3 times (9 sts).

Row 4: ch 1, turn, *sc in next 2 sts, 2 sc in next st* 3 times (12 sts).

Row 5: ch 1, turn, *sc in next 3 sts, 2 sc in next st* 3 times (15 sts).

Rows 6-7: ch 1, turn, sc in each st across.

Row 8: ch 1, do not turn, work 11 sc across Edge A referrring to picture below (11 sts). Fasten off.

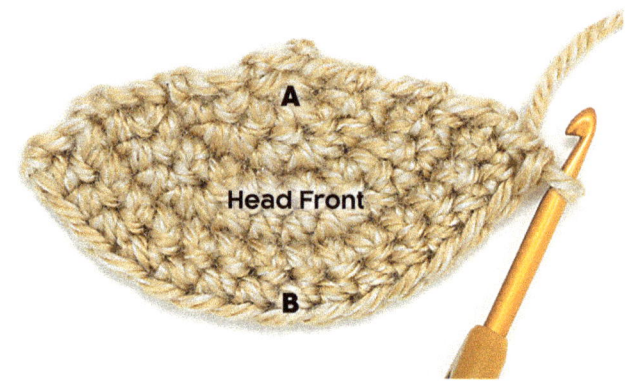

Place the 2 Head Front pieces with wrong sides facing and sew together along Edge B. This edge will be the Camel's lips.

Sew Head Front to Head Back pausing to stuff when pieces are nearly connected. Squeeze Head into shape.

NOSE

With tan yarn, ch 2.

Row 1: 2 sc in 2nd ch from hook (2 sts).

Row 2: ch 1, turn, 2 sc in each st across (4 sts).

Row 3: ch 1, turn, sc in each st across.

Row 4: ch 1, turn, 2 sc in next st, sc in next 2 sts, 2 sc in next st (6 sts).

Row 5: ch 1, turn, sc in each st across. Fasten off.

EARS (MAKE 2)

The ears are worked around a foundation chain.

EAR FRONT

With tan yarn, ch 4.

Rnd 1: starting in 2nd ch from hook, sc in next 2 chs, 3 sc in last ch, sc in next 2 ch (7 sts).

Rnd 2: ch 1, turn, sc in next 3 sts, 3 sc in next st, sc in next 3 sts (9 sts). Fasten off.

EAR BACK

With tan yarn, ch 4.

Rnd 1: starting in 2nd ch from hook, sc in next 2 chs, 3 sc in last ch, sc in next 2 ch (7 sts).

Rnd 2: ch 1, turn, sc in next 3 sts, 3 sc in next st, sc in next 3 sts (9 sts).

Rnd 3: ch 1, turn, place Ear Front against Ear Back with wrong sides facing and sts aligned. Working thru both layers, sc in next 4 sts, 3 sc in next st, sc in next 4 sts (11 sts).

Rnd 4: ch 1, turn, sc in next 5 sts, 3 sc in next st, sc in next 5 sts (13 sts). Fasten off.

Sew first 3 tails into space between layers of Ear to hide them, cut off excess. Thread remaining tail in yarn needle, sew into opposite corner and pull tight. This will connect the corners and shape the Ear. Secure with a stitch and knot.

Pinch tip of Ear into a point.

BRIDLE

BRIDLE BACK

With red yarn, ch 31.

Row 1: ch 1, turn, sc in each st across (31 sts).

Row 2: for **points**, ch 1, turn, sl st in first 3 sts, *ch 3 loosely, sl st in back bar of 3rd ch from hook, skip 1 st, sl st in next 3 sts* across. Fasten off.

BRIDLE FRONT

With red yarn, ch 30.

Row 1: ch 1, turn, sc in each st across (30 sts). Fasten off.

FINISHING

Sew Nose to top of Head Front.

Glue on eyes between Rnds 10-11 of Head Back with an interspace of 8-9 sts.

Sew on Ears as shown in picture.

With a double strand of black yarn, embroider a "Y" on Head Front as shown in picture.

Sew Bridle Back and Bridle Front to Head with wrong sides out, Sew a button on each side where Bridle Front meets Bridle Back. Glue on jewels.

For **tassels**, cut 6" lengths of yarn in purple, green and turquoise. Alternating the colors, attach 2 strands in each point of Bridle Back as follows: Insert hook thru st, holding 2 strands together, pull centers of strands part way thru st to make a loop, feed ends of yarn thru loop and pull loop tight. Trim ends to 1".

Attach jump ring (see page 80).

Polar Bear

A black animal eye can be substituted for the triangle nose if desired.

SUPPLIES

G6/4mm crochet hook
Worsted weight yarn in white
2 black safety eyes, 8mm
Black triangle animal nose, 10mm
Glue (see page 8)
Polyester fiberfill stuffing
Jump ring, 10mm

HEAD

With white yarn, make a magic ring, ch 1.

Rnd 1: 6 sc in ring, pull ring closed tight (6 sts).

Rnd 2: *sc in next st, 2 sc in next st* 3 times. Place marker for beginning of rnd and move marker up as each rnd is completed (9 sts).

Rnd 3: *sc in next 2 sts, 2 sc in next st* 3 times (12 sts).

Rnd 4: *sc in next 2 sts, 2 sc in next st* 4 times (16 sts).

Rnd 5: *sc in next 3 sts, 2 sc in next st* 4 times (20 sts).

Rnd 6: *sc in next 4 sts, 2 sc in next st* 4 times (24 sts).

Rnd 7: *sc in next 5 sts, 2 sc in next st* 4 times (28 sts).

Rnd 8: *sc in next 6 sts, 2 sc in next st* 4 times (32 sts).

Rnd 9: *sc in next 7 sts, 2 sc in next st* 4 times (36 sts).

Rnds 10-16: sc in each st around.

Start to stuff and continue stuffing after each round.

Rnd 17: *sc in next 4 sts, invdec* 6 times (30 sts).

Rnd 18: *sc in next 3 sts, invdec* 6 times (24 sts).

Rnd 19: *sc in next 2 sts, invdec* 6 times (18 sts).

Rnd 20: *sc in next st, invdec* 6 times (12 sts).

Rnd 21: invdec 6 times (6 sts).

Fasten off. Finish adding stuffing.

To close hole, thread tail in yarn needle, insert needle thru front loop of each st around opening and pull tight. Weave in end. Squeeze Head into shape.

EARS (MAKE 2)

Make a magic ring, ch 1.

Rnd 1: 6 sc in ring, pull ring closed tight (6 sts).

Rnd 2: 2 sc in each st around. Place marker for beginning of rnd and move marker up as each rnd is completed (12 sts).

Rnds 3-5: sc in each st around. Fasten off.

FINISHING

Glue on eyes between Rnds 10-11 with an interspace of 6-7 sts.

Sew Ears slightly cupped on Rnd 16 of Head.

Glue on nose at edge of Rnd 1.

Attach jump ring (see page 80).

Cat

If you have a special cat in your life, it would be fun to make an ornament in matching colors.

SUPPLIES

G6/4mm crochet hook

Worsted weight yarn in brown, gold, pink, and white

2 green slit-pupil safety eyes, 10mm

Glue (see page 8)

Polyester fiberfill stuffing

Jump ring, 10mm

Note: A chain 1 at the beginning of a rnd is for turning your work and does not count as a stitch.

HEAD

The Head is made by alternating 2 rnds of brown with 2 rnds of gold. **Change to alternate color in last st of every other rnd.**

Make a magic ring, ch 1.

Rnd 1: 6 sc in ring, pull ring closed tight (6 sts).

Rnd 2: 2 sc in each st around. Place marker for beginning of rnd and move marker up as each rnd is completed (12 sts).

Rnd 3: *sc in next st, 2 sc in next st* 6 times (18 sts).

Rnd 4: *sc in next 2 sts, 2 sc in next st* 6 times (24 sts).

Rnd 5: *sc in next 3 sts, 2 sc in next st* 6 times (30 sts).

Rnd 6: *sc in next 4 sts, 2 sc in next st* 6 times (36 sts).

Rnds 7-13: sc in each st around.

Rnd 14: *sc in next 4 sts, invdec* 6 times (30 sts).

Rnd 15: *sc in next 3 sts, invdec* 6 times (24 sts).

Start to stuff and continue stuffing after each rnd.

Rnd 16: *sc in next 2 sts, invdec* 6 times (18 sts).

Rnd 17: *sc in next st, invdec* 6 times (12 sts).

Rnd 18: invdec 6 times (6 sts).

Fasten off. Finish adding stuffing.

To close hole, thread tail in yarn needle, insert needle thru front loop of each st around opening and pull tight. Weave in end. Squeeze Head into a nice round shape.

EARS (MAKE 2)

The ears are worked around a foundation chain.

EAR FRONT

With pink yarn, ch 4.

Rnd 1: starting in 2nd ch from hook, sc in next 2 chs, 3 sc in last ch, sc in next 2 ch (7 sts). Fasten off.

EAR BACK

With brown yarn, ch 4.

Rnd 1: starting in 2nd ch from hook, sc in next 2 chs, 3 sc in last ch, sc in next 2 ch (7 sts).

Rnd 2: ch 1, turn, place Ear Front against Ear Back with wrong sides facing and sts aligned. Working thru both layers, sc in next 3 sts, 3 sc in next st, sc in next 3 sts (9 sts).

Rnd 3: ch 1, turn, sc in next 4 sts, 3 sc in next st, sc in next 4 sts (11 sts).

Rnd 4: ch 1, turn, sc in next 5 sts, 3 sc in next st, sc in next 5 sts (13 sts). Fasten off.

Sew first 3 tails into space between layers of Ear to hide them, cut off excess.

Pinch tip of Ear into a point.

FINISHING

Glue on eyes between Rnds 9-10 of Head with an interspace of 6-7 sts.

Sew Ears with rims cupped on top of Head: place inner edges on groove between Rnds 2-3.

For **nose**, embroider 5 straight sts with pink yarn as shown in picture: make sts thru the same crochet st at the bottom to form a point.

For **whiskers**, embroider straight sts with white yarn as shown in picture.

Attach jump ring (see page 80).

Dog

SUPPLIES

G6/4mm crochet hook

Worsted weight yarn in tan and black

2 black safety eyes, 8mm

Black triangle animal nose, 10mm

Glue (see page 8)

Polyester fiberfill stuffing

Jump ring, 10mm

Note: A chain 1 at the beginning of a row is for turning your work and does not count as a stitch.

HEAD

With tan yarn, make a magic ring, ch 1.

Rnd 1: 6 sc in ring, pull ring closed tight (6 sts).

Rnd 2: 2 sc in each st around. Place marker for beginning of rnd and move marker up as each rnd is completed (12 sts).

Rnd 3: *sc in next st, 2 sc in next st* 6 times (18 sts).

Rnds 4-6: sc in each st around.

Rnd 7: *sc in next 2 sts, 2 sc in next st* 6 times (24 sts).

Rnd 8: *sc in next 3 sts, 2 sc in next st* 6 times (30 sts).

Rnd 9: *sc in next 4 sts, 2 sc in next st* 6 times (36 sts).

Rnds 10-16: sc in each st around.

Rnd 17: *sc in next 4 sts, invdec* 6 times (30 sts).

Rnd 18: *sc in next 3 sts, invdec* 6 times (24 sts).

Start to stuff and continue stuffing after each rnd.

Rnd 19: *sc in next 2 sts, invdec* 6 times (18 sts).

Rnd 20: *sc in next st, invdec* 6 times (12 sts).

Rnd 21: invdec 6 times (6 sts).

Fasten off. Finish adding stuffing.

To close hole, thread tail in yarn needle, insert needle thru front loop of each st around opening and pull tight. Weave in end. Squeeze Head into shape.

EARS (MAKE 2)

With tan yarn, ch 6.

Rows 1-6: ch 1, turn, sc in each st across (6 sts).

Note: The remaining rows do not have a turning ch.

Row 7: turn, skip first st, sc in each remaining st across (5 sts).

Row 8: turn, skip first st, sc in each remaining st across (4 sts).

Row 9: turn, skip first st, sc in each remaining st across (3 sts).

Row 10: turn, skip first st, sc in each remaining st across (2 sts).

Row 11: turn, skip first st, sc in next st (1 st).

Rnd 12: sc around perimeter making 3 sts in same st at top corners (see blue dots). Sl st in next st. Fasten off.

FINISHING

Glue on eyes between Rnds 7-8 with an interspace of 5-6 sts. With black yarn, embroider a st from center of Rnd 1 to groove between Rnds 2-3 as pictured. Glue on nose at center of Rnd 1. Place front corners of Ears on Rnd 13 of Head and angle the back corners so Ears hang as shown in picture. Sew in place. Weave in ends.

Attach jump ring (see page 80).

Penguin

SUPPLIES

G6/4mm crochet hook

Worsted weight yarn in white, black and orange

2 black safety eyes, 8mm

Glue (see page 8)

Polyester fiberfill stuffing

Jump ring, 10mm

Note: A chain 1 at the beginning of a row is for turning your work and does not count as a stitch.

HEAD

With white yarn, make a magic ring, ch 1.

Rnd 1: 6 sc in ring, pull ring closed tight (6 sts).

Rnd 2: 2 sc in each st around. Place marker for beginning of rnd and move marker up as each rnd is completed (12 sts).

Rnd 3: *sc in next st, 2 sc in next st* 6 times (18 sts).

Rnd 4: *sc in next 2 sts, 2 sc in next st* 6 times (24 sts).

Rnd 5: *sc in next 3 sts, 2 sc in next st* 6 times (30 sts).

Rnd 6: *sc in next 4 sts, 2 sc in next st* 6 times (36 sts).

Rnd 7: sc in each st around; change to black yarn in last st.

Rnd 8: sc in each st around.

Rnd 9: working in **back loops only**, sc in each st around.

Rnds 10-13: resuming work in **both loops**, sc in each st around.

Rnd 14: *sc in next 4 sts, invdec* 6 times (30 sts).

Rnd 15: *sc in next 3 sts, invdec* 6 times (24 sts).

Start to stuff and continue stuffing after each rnd.

Rnd 16: *sc in next 2 sts, invdec* 6 times (18 sts).

Rnd 17: *sc in next st, invdec* 6 times (12 sts).

Rnd 18: invdec 6 times (6 sts).

Fasten off. Finish adding stuffing.

To close hole, thread tail in yarn needle, insert needle thru front loop of each st around opening and pull tight. Weave in end.

Squeeze Head into a nice round shape.

WIDOW'S PEAK

The Widow's Peak is made in unworked front loops of Rnd 9 of Head. Mark 7 sts for its position as follows: In white "face" area of Head, you should see faint grooves radiating out from the center that outline 6 pie-shaped sections. Choose section with jog from color change and work Widow's Peak there.

Hold Head with black side facing you.

Row 1: With black yarn and an 18" starting tail, join with sc in first marked st, sc in next 6 sts (7 sts).

Row 2: ch 1, turn, sc2tog, sc in next 5 sts (6 sts).

Row 3: ch 1, turn, sc2tog, sc in next 4 sts (5 sts).

Row 4: ch 1, turn, sc2tog, sc in next 3 sts (4 sts).

Row 5: ch 1, turn, sc2tog, sc in next 2 sts (3 sts).

Row 6: ch 1, turn, sc2tog, sc in next st (2 sts).

Row 7: ch 1, turn, sc2tog (1 st).

Next you will make a neat finish along the edges.

Row 8: work forward and sc along next side of Widow's Peak. Fasten off. Weave in end.

Row 9: pull up a loop with starting tail and sc along remaining side of Widow's Peak. Fasten off.

Sew ending tail into Head to attach tip of Widow's Peak as shown in picture.

FINISHING

Glue on eyes between Rnds 4-5 so that top edges are aligned with tip of Widow's Peak. For **beak**, embroider 5 straight sts with orange yarn as shown in picture: make sts thru the same crochet st at the bottom to form a point.

Attach jump ring (see page 80).

Baby's First Christmas

The keepsake baby ornaments are personalized with Baby's name and birth date. Instructions are provided for easy tape-laminated tags that are sewn to the back. Another option is to purchase engraved metal charms. Search Etsy for Custom Laser Engraved Charm and you will find many economical sources.

Baby Girl

SUPPLIES

G6/4mm crochet hook

Worsted weight yarn in beige, pink, black & desired hair color

Hot glue

Polyester fiberfill stuffing

Paper or cardstock

Package tape

Hole punches, 1/8" and 1"

Small amount of 3/8" pink ribbon

Serving fork

Jump ring, 10mm

HEAD

With beige yarn, make a magic ring, ch 1.

Rnd 1: 6 sc in ring, pull ring closed tight (6 sts).

Rnd 2: 2 sc in each st around. Place marker for beginning of rnd and move marker up as each rnd is completed (12 sts).

Rnd 3: *sc in next st, 2 sc in next st* 6 times (18 sts).

Rnd 4: *sc in next 2 sts, 2 sc in next st* 6 times (24 sts).

Rnd 5: *sc in next 3 sts, 2 sc in next st* 6 times (30 sts).

Rnd 6: *sc in next 4 sts, 2 sc in next st* 6 times (36 sts).

Rnds 7-13: sc in each st around.

Rnd 14: *sc in next 4 sts, invdec* 6 times (30 sts).

Rnd 15: *sc in next 3 sts, invdec* 6 times (24 sts).

Start to stuff and continue stuffing after each rnd.

Rnd 16: *sc in next 2 sts, invdec* 6 times (18 sts).

Rnd 17: *sc in next st, invdec* 6 times (12 sts).

Rnd 18: invdec 6 times (6 sts).

Fasten off. Finish adding stuffing.

To close hole, thread tail in yarn needle, insert needle thru front loop of each st around opening and pull tight. Weave in end.

Squeeze Head into a nice round shape.

BONNET

With pink yarn, make a magic ring, ch 1.

Rnd 1: 6 sc in ring, pull ring closed tight (6 sts).

Rnd 2: 2 sc in each st around. Place marker for beginning of rnd and move marker up as each rnd is completed (12 sts).

Rnd 3: *sc in next st, 2 sc in next st* 6 times (18 sts).

Rnd 4: *sc in next 2 sts, 2 sc in next st* 6 times (24 sts).

Rnd 5: *sc in next 3 sts, 2 sc in next st* 6 times (30 sts).

Rnd 6: *sc in next 4 sts, 2 sc in next st* 6 times (36 sts).

Rnd 7: *sc in next 5 sts, 2 sc in next st* 6 times (42 sts).

Rnds 8-13: sc in each st around.

Rnd 14: *sc in next 5 sts, invdec* 6 times, join with sl st in first st (36 sts).

Rnd 15: ch 4, tr in each st around, join with sl st in 3rd ch of starting ch-4. Fasten off. Weave in ends.

HAIR CURL

With yarn in desired hair color, ch 15, turn, sc in 2nd ch from hook and in each remaining ch across. Fasten off.

FINISHING

Using black yarn, embroider **eyes** on Rnd 9 with an interspace of 5 sts: Bring needle out at Point A, insert needle at Point B leaving the yarn loose to shape the eye. Bring needle out again at Point C, go over the loose strand and insert needle back in at Point C. Pull yarn gently, just until eye lays flat. Secure ends inside Head.

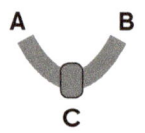

With beige yarn, embroider **nose** 2 rows below eyes.

Sew Hair Curl to Head by sewing tails down into Rnd 1. Glue Curl in place if desired.

For **ribbon trim**, thread ribbon in yarn needle. Starting at join in Rnd 15 of Bonnet, weave ribbon thru tr sts. Place Bonnet on Head to adjust fit, knot ribbon and tuck ends inside Bonnet. Sew Bonnet to Head as pictured.

For **bow**, cut a 10" strand of ribbon.

1. Wrap ribbon around fork so that 1 end is laying in front and 1 in back (see Ends A and B below).

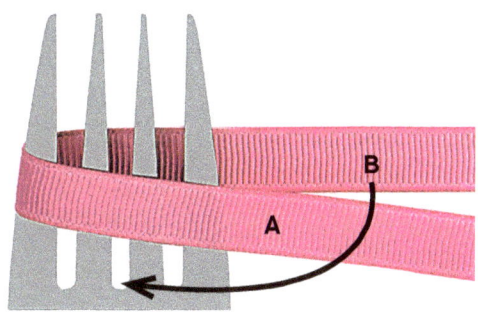

2. Take End B, bring it around to front and insert it between middle 2 tines BELOW End A.

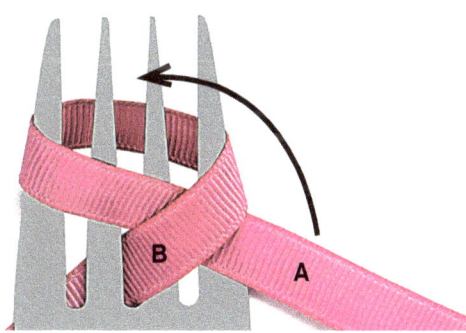

3. Take End A and insert it between middle 2 tines ABOVE rest of ribbon in front ...

... to look like photo below.

4. Turn fork over and tie ends together tightly with a simple knot (1 time around).

5. Remove bow from fork and trim ends to desired length. Cut ends at an angle as shown in picture. This will discourage fraying. To <u>prevent</u> fraying, apply Fray Check or clear nail polish to edges. Another method is to sweep edges along a flame to melt the fibers.

Attach bow to lower edge of Bonnet with hot glue.

For **name tag**, hand-write or print from computer the baby's name and birth date onto paper or cardstock. Cover both sides with package tape. Cut into a 1" circle or use a 1" punch. Punch a small hole at top and sew to center back of ornament.

Attach jump ring (see page 80).

BABY BOY

SUPPLIES

G6/4mm crochet hook

Worsted weight yarn in beige, 2 blues, black & desired hair color

Polyester fiberfill stuffing

Paper or cardstock

Package tape

Hole punches, 1/8" and 1"

Small amount of 3/8" blue ribbon

Serving fork

Jump ring, 10mm

HEAD

With beige yarn, make a magic ring, ch 1.

Rnd 1: 6 sc in ring, pull ring closed tight (6 sts).

Rnd 2: 2 sc in each st around. Place marker for beginning of rnd and move marker up as each rnd is completed (12 sts).

Rnd 3: *sc in next st, 2 sc in next st* 6 times (18 sts).

Rnd 4: *sc in next 2 sts, 2 sc in next st* 6 times (24 sts).

Rnd 5: *sc in next 3 sts, 2 sc in next st* 6 times (30 sts).

Rnd 6: *sc in next 4 sts, 2 sc in next st* 6 times (36 sts).

Rnds 7-13: sc in each st around.

Rnd 14: *sc in next 4 sts, invdec* 6 times (30 sts).

Rnd 15: *sc in next 3 sts, invdec* 6 times (24 sts).

Start to stuff and continue stuffing after each rnd.

Rnd 16: *sc in next 2 sts, invdec* 6 times (18 sts).

Rnd 17: *sc in next st, invdec* 6 times (12 sts).

Rnd 18: invdec 6 times (6 sts).

Fasten off. Finish adding stuffing.

To close hole, thread tail in yarn needle, insert needle thru front loop of each st around opening and pull tight. Weave in end.

Squeeze Head into a nice round shape.

BEANIE

With blue yarn, make a magic ring, ch 1.

Rnd 1: 6 sc in ring, pull ring closed tight (6 sts).

Rnd 2: 2 sc in each st around. Place marker for beginning of rnd and move marker up as each rnd is completed (12 sts).

Rnd 3: *sc in next st, 2 sc in next st* 6 times (18 sts).

Rnd 4: *sc in next 2 sts, 2 sc in next st* 6 times (24 sts).

Rnd 5: *sc in next 3 sts, 2 sc in next st* 6 times (30 sts).

Rnd 6: *sc in next 4 sts, 2 sc in next st* 6 times (36 sts).

Rnd 7: *sc in next 5 sts, 2 sc in next st* 6 times (42 sts).

Rnds 8-13: sc in each st around.

Rnd 14: *sc in next 5 sts, invdec* 6 times, join with sl st in first st (36 sts).

Rnd 15: ch 4, tr in each st around, join with sl st in 3rd ch of starting ch-4. Fasten off. Weave in ends.

HAIR CURL

With yarn in desired hair color, ch 15, turn, sc in 2nd ch from hook and in each remaining ch across. Fasten off.

FINISHING

Using black yarn, embroider **eyes** on Rnd 9 with an interspace of 5 sts: Bring needle out at Point A, insert needle at Point B leaving the yarn loose to shape the eye. Bring needle out again at Point C, go over the loose strand and insert needle back in at Point C. Pull yarn gently, just until eye lays flat. Secure ends inside Head.

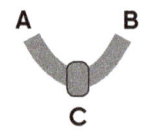

With beige yarn, embroider **nose** 2 rows below eyes.

Sew Hair Curl to Head by sewing tails down into Rnd 1. Glue Curl in place if desired.

For **ribbon trim**, thread ribbon in yarn needle. Starting at join in Rnd 15 of Beanie, weave ribbon thru tr sts. Place Beanie on Head to adjust fit, knot ribbon and tuck ends inside Beanie. Sew Beanie to Head at an angle as pictured.

For **pom pom**, use a different shade of blue than used for Beanie.

1. Wrap yarn around fork 50 times. Cut yarn.

2. Cut a 12" piece of yarn and tie it around middle of bundle. Knot tightly. Wrap tails to opposite side and knot tightly again.

For **name tag**, hand-write or print from computer the baby's name and birth date onto paper or cardstock. Cover both sides with package tape. Cut into a 1" circle or use a 1" punch. Punch a small hole at top and sew to center back of ornament.

3. Remove yarn from fork and cut loops open. Fluff yarn with fingers—then trim yarn until pom pom is nicely rounded. Just trim a little bit at a time.

Note: Do not trim the long strand used for tying the yarn bundle. Save this for sewing pom pom to Beanie.

Sew pom pom to Rnd 1 of Beanie.

Attach jump ring (see page 80).

STITCHES

SLIP KNOT

This is used to make a starting loop on the crochet hook.

1. Make a loop about 5 inches from end of yarn. Insert hook in loop and hook onto supply yarn (yarn coming from ball) at A.

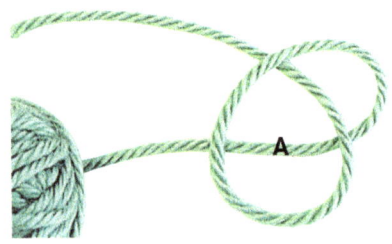

2. Pull yarn through loop.

3. Pull yarn ends to tighten loop around hook.

SLIP STITCH (SL ST)

1. Insert hook in stitch. Yarn over and pull through stitch and through loop on hook (A and B).

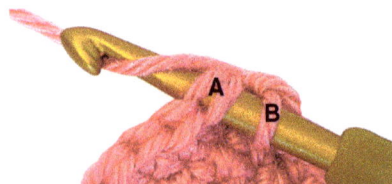

2. The sl st is done.

CHAIN (CH)

Start with a slip knot on hook.

1. Bring yarn **over** hook from back to front. Catch yarn with hook and pull it through the loop —

to look like this. One ch is done.

SINGLE CROCHET (SC)

This simple stitch is the primary stitch for amigurumi.

1. Insert hook in designated stitch. Note: Put hook under **both loops** that form v-shape at top of stitch unless otherwise instructed.

2. Yarn over and pull through the stitch (A).

You now have 2 loops on the hook:

3. Yarn over and pull through both loops on hook.

4. You now have 1 loop on hook and the sc stitch is done.

HALF DOUBLE CROCHET (HDC)

1. Yarn over and insert hook in designated stitch.

2. Yarn over and pull through the stitch (A).

You now have 3 loops on hook:

3. Yarn over and pull through all 3 loops on hook (A, B & C).

4. You now have 1 loop on hook and the hdc stitch is done.

DOUBLE CROCHET (DC)

1. Yarn over and insert hook in designated stitch.

2. Yarn over and pull through the stitch (A).

You now have 3 loops on hook:

3. Yarn over and pull through 1st 2 loops on hook (A and B).

You now have 2 loops on hook:

4. Yarn over and pull through both loops on hook.

5. You now have 1 loop on hook and the dc stitch is done.

TRIPLE OR TREBLE CROCHET (TR)

1. Yarn over twice and insert hook in designated stitch.

2. Yarn over and pull thru the st. There are now 4 loops on hook.

3. Yarn over and pull thru **1st two loops** on hook. There are now 3 loops on hook.

4. Yarn over and pull thru **next two loops** on hook.

5. Yarn over and pull yarn thru **last two loops** on hook. There is now 1 loop on hook and the tr stitch is done.

LOOP STITCH (LP ST)

The Loop Stitch is a variation of single crochet. The loops will form on the wrong side of the fabric (the side opposite the side you are facing).

1. Insert hook in designated stitch, just as you do for a single crochet.

2. Wrap yarn around index finger of your yarn-holding hand to make a loop and lay loop on top of hook. Pull strands A and B thru stitch C.

3. Yarn over and pull through all 3 loops on hook—A, B, and C.

4. The lp st is done.

77

SINGLE CROCHET 2 TOGETHER (SC2TOG)

This is a common way to decrease 2 stitches into 1 stitch. It is easy and effective but it can leave a slight bump and gap. You can substitute invdec if desired.

1. Insert hook in stitch, yarn over and pull up a loop — to look like this:

2. Insert hook in next stitch, yarn over and pull up a loop — to look like this:

3. Yarn over and pull through all 3 loops on hook — to look like this. The sc2tog is done.

INVISIBLE DECREASE (INVDEC)

This is a very neat way to decrease 2 sts into 1 st. I used it for most of my decreases in this book. You can substitute sc2tog if desired.

1. Insert hook in **front loop** of 1st st. DO NOT YARN OVER. You now have 2 loops on hook.

2. Insert hook in **front loop** of next st. You now have 3 loops on hook.

3. Yarn over and pull thru 1st 2 loops on hook. You now have 2 loops on hook.

3. Yarn over and pull thru both loops on hook. The invdec is done.

TECHNIQUES

★ MAGIC RING

Most all of my amigurumi begins with the magic ring. This is an adjustable loop that makes a neat center when crocheting in the round. If you're not familiar with it, you may want to watch a YouTube tutorial. It's not difficult — and well worth it.

An alternative to the magic ring, if desired, is to ch 2; then begin Rnd 1 by working the required number of sts as stated in the pattern in 2nd ch from hook. This method will leave a small hole in the middle of the first round (see photos below).

Magic Ring

Ch 2

Make the Magic Ring as follows:

1. Make a ring a few inches from end of yarn. Grasp ring between thumb and index finger where the join makes an X. Insert hook in ring, hook onto supply yarn at Y and pull up a loop —

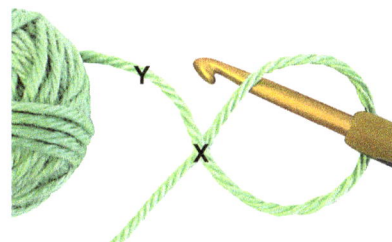

to look like this.

2. Chain 1 —

to look like this. This chain does not count as a stitch.

3. Insert hook into ring so you're crocheting over ring and yarn tail. Pull up a loop to begin your first single crochet —

and complete the single crochet.

4. Continue to crochet over ring and yarn tail for the specified number of single crochets for the 1st round.

5. Pull tail to close up ring. To begin the 2nd round, insert hook in 1st stitch of 1st round (see arrow).

BEGIN 2ND RND HERE

WORKING IN THE ROUND

Working in the round is crocheting in a continuous spiral. Lots of amigurumi is worked this way.

WORKING IN LOOPS

When a single crochet stitch is made, you will see 2 loops in a v-shape at the top of the stitch. To crochet the patterns in this book, insert your hook under **both loops** unless instructed otherwise. Crocheting in the "front loops only" or the "back loops only" is sometimes used for a different effect.

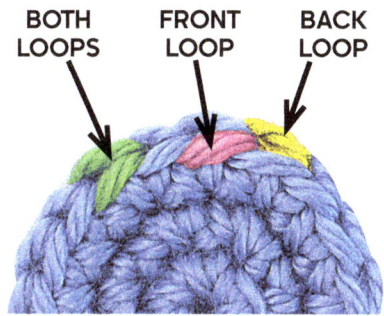
BOTH LOOPS   FRONT LOOP   BACK LOOP

CHANGING COLORS

To change color while single crocheting, work last stitch of old color to last yarn over, yarn over with new color and pull through both loops to complete the stitch.

79

ROTATING YOUR HOOK

When you wrap yarn over your hook, the front of the hook should be facing you. Then when it's time to pull the yarn through the loop on the hook, rotate the hook downward. It will slide easily through the loop instead of getting caught.

COUNTING ROUNDS

Periodically, it is good to count your rounds to ensure your place in a pattern. Fortunately, rounds are clearly defined and counting is easy. Each round makes a ridge. A groove separates the rounds. You need only to count the ridges. Take a look at the photo below to see that the circle has 5 rounds.

USING STITCH MARKERS

It can be tricky to keep track of your place when working in the round, so be sure to use a stitch marker. Place the stitch marker in the first stitch of a round — after completing the stitch. When you've crocheted all the way around, remove the stitch marker, make the next stitch, and replace the marker in the stitch just made. This will be the first stitch of the next round.

FASTENING OFF

This is the way to finish a piece so that it won't unravel. When you're done crocheting, cut the yarn and leave a tail. Wrap the tail over your hook and pull it all the way through the last loop left on your hook. Pull the tail tight and it will make a knot.

JOINING YARN

To join new yarn onto a crocheted item, such as to make a border or an appendage to an applique, insert hook in desired stitch, make a loop and pull it through the stitch.

JOINING WITH SL ST

Start with a Slip Knot on hook. Insert hook in specified stitch. Yarn over and pull through the stitch and the loop on the hook.

JOINING WITH SC

Put yarn on hook with a Slip Knot. Insert hook in indicated stitch. Complete sc as shown in Single Crochet tutorial, page 76, steps 2-4.

ASSEMBLING

The assembly of amigurumi is an exciting step! Take your time and pin the parts in place by referring to the pictures of the finished project. Use care and an eye for symmetry. Thread a yarn needle with the tail of your auxiliary piece (ear, antler, hat, etc.) and use a whip stitch or running stitch to sew it in place. A sewing needle and thread can also be used to sew your parts together. In some cases, this will make the stitches less visible.

WEAVING IN ENDS

The instruction to "weave in ends" is included in every pattern. This is the way to hide and secure all of your straggly yarn tails. For a stuffed shape, it's very easy. Thread yarn tail into a yarn needle, poke needle into object, push thru stuffing, and come out at another location. Cut yarn flush with stuffie and squeeze to make any visible tail retract inside. For flat pieces, follow this "Rule of 3": (1) Thread yarn tail into a yarn needle, skim thru back of sts on wrong side of work for a short distance; (2) turn and go in opposite direction thru different sts; (3) turn and go in original direction to lock the yarn in place. Trim end close. When you turn to the right side, you should not see the woven ends. They should be tucked into the middle of your crocheted fabric.

ATTACHING JUMP RINGS

Determine the location for an ornament's jump ring by finding where it balances best. You can do this by going under a stitch with your crochet hook, yarn needle or stitch marker. To attach ring, hold with its "cut" facing upward. Grasp ring firmly along each side with fingers or small pliers. Twist ring open from front-to-back. (Do not twist from side-to-side as this will stretch out the shape.) Slide ring under yarn at desired location. To close ring, twist back and wiggle until ends meet. Jump rings can be sewn to an ornament if preferred.

Resources

YARN

Amazon
amazon.com

Herrschners
herrschners.com

Joann Fabric and Craft Stores
joann.com

Lovecrafts
lovecrafts.com

NOTIONS

Amazon
amazon.com

Joann Fabric and Craft Stores
joann.com

SAFETY EYES

Amazon
amazon.com

CR's Crafts
crscrafts.com

Etsy Shop 6060
etsy.com/shop/6060

Glass Eyes Online
glasseyesonline.com

VIDEO TUTORIALS

youtube.com
Search on the name of the stitch or technique you want to learn.

Pinterest
pinterest.com/LindalooEnt/
Visit my Pinterest page to view video tutorials for the stitches and techniques used in this book. Look for the board named "Amigurumi Tutorials".

Yarn

The following yarns were used for these projects.

NATIVITY SET

Star of Bethlehem (Worsted, #4)
    Lion Brand "Vanna's Choice", Mustard

Baby Jesus (Worsted, #4)
    Lion Brand "Vanna's Choice", Beige
    Lion Brand "Vanna's Choice", Fisherman

Mary (Worsted, #4)
    Lion Brand "Vanna's Choice", Beige
    Lion Brand "Vanna's Choice", Raspberry
    Red Heart "Soft", Toast

Joseph (Worsted, #4)
    Lion Brand "Vanna's Choice", Beige
    Lion Brand "Vanna's Choice", Dusty Blue
    Lion Brand "Vanna's Choice", Chocolate
    Lion Brand "Vanna's Choice", Fisherman

Angel (Worsted, #4)
    Lion Brand "Vanna's Choice", Beige
    Lion Brand "Vanna's Choice", Lemon

Shepherd (Worsted, #4)
    Lion Brand "Vanna's Choice", Beige
    Lion Brand "Vanna's Choice", Taupe
    Lion Brand "Vanna's Choice", Dusty Green
    Lion Brand "Vanna's Choice", Cranberry

Wiseman I (Worsted, #4)
    Lion Brand "Vanna's Choice", Beige
    Lion Brand "Vanna's Choice", Silver Heather
    Lion Brand "Vanna's Choice", Honey
    Lion Brand "Vanna's Choice", Peacock

Wiseman II (Worsted, #4)
    Red Heart "Soft", Wheat
    Lion Brand "Vanna's Choice", Charcoal Grey
    Lion Brand "Vanna's Choice", Mustard
    Lion Brand "Vanna's Choice", Cranberry

Wiseman III (Worsted, #4)
    Red Heart "Super Saver", Cafe Latte
    Lion Brand "Vanna's Choice", Dark Grey Heather
    Lion Brand "Vanna's Choice", Eggplant
    Lion Brand "Vanna's Choice", Dusty Purple

Ox (Worsted, #4)
    Lion Brand "Vanna's Choice", Rust
    Lion Brand "Vanna's Choice", Beige
    Lion Brand "Vanna's Choice", Black

Donkey (Worsted, #4)
    Lion Brand "Vanna's Choice", Silver Grey
    Lion Brand "Vanna's Choice", Pale Grey
    Lion Brand "Vanna's Choice", Black

Sheep (Worsted, #4)
    Lion Brand "Vanna's Choice", Fisherman
    Lion Brand "Vanna's Choice", Pink
    Lion Brand "Vanna's Choice", Black

NORTH POLE CHARACTERS

Santa Claus (Worsted, #4)
    Lion Brand "Vanna's Choice", Beige
    Lion Brand "Vanna's Choice", Fisherman
    Lion Brand "Vanna's Choice", Cranberry

Mrs. Claus (Worsted, #4)
    Lion Brand "Vanna's Choice", Beige
    Lion Brand "Vanna's Choice", Silver Heather
    (DK, Light Worsted, #3)
    Stylecraft "Special DK", Lipstick
    Stylecraft "Special DK", Kelly Green

Reindeer (Worsted, #4)
    Lion Brand "Heartland", Grand Canyon
    Lion Brand "Heartland", Mammoth Cave
    Lion Brand "Heartland", Acadia
    Lion Brand "Heartland", Redwood

Elf (Worsted, #4)
    Lion Brand "Vanna's Choice", Beige
    Lion Brand "Vanna's Choice", Chocolate
    Lion Brand "Vanna's Choice", Fern
    Lion Brand "Vanna's Choice", Cranberry
    Lion Brand "Vanna's Choice", Mustard

Snowman (Worsted, #4)
    Lion Brand "Vanna's Choice", Fisherman
    Lion Brand "Vanna's Choice", Black
    Lion Brand "Vanna's Choice", Sky Blue
    Lion Brand "Vanna's Choice", Terracotta

Gingerbread Man (Worsted, #4)
    Lion Brand "Vanna's Choice", Fisherman
    Lion Brand "Vanna's Choice", Honey
    Lion Brand "Vanna's Choice", Cranberry
    Lion Brand "Vanna's Choice", Fern

Toy Soldier (Worsted, #4)
    Lion Brand "Vanna's Choice", Beige
    Lion Brand "Vanna's Choice", Sky Blue
    Lion Brand "Vanna's Choice", Mustard
    Lion Brand "Vanna's Choice", Cranberry
    Lion Brand "Vanna's Choice", Fisherman

SWEET TREATS

Candy Cane (Worsted, #4)
    Lion Brand "Vanna's Choice", Fisherman
    Lion Brand "Vanna's Choice", Scarlet

Mistletoe Truffle (Worsted, #4)
    Lion Brand "Vanna's Choice", Fisherman
    Lion Brand "Vanna's Choice", Fern
    Lion Brand "Vanna's Choice", Scarlet
    Lion Brand "Vanna's Choice", Chocolate

Snow Cone (Worsted, #4)
    Lion Brand "Vanna's Choice", Fisherman
    Lion Brand "Vanna's Choice", Grapefruit
    Lion Brand "Vanna's Choice", Pistachio
    Lion Brand "Vanna's Choice", Sky Blue
    Loops & Threads "Impeccable", Sunny Day

Snowflake Macaron (Worsted, #4)
    Lion Brand "Vanna's Choice", Fisherman
    Lion Brand "Vanna's Choice", Sky Blue

Ribbon Candy (Worsted, #4)
    Lion Brand "Vanna's Choice", Fisherman
    Lion Brand "Vanna's Choice", Grapefruit
    Lion Brand "Vanna's Choice", Fern

Starlight Peppermint (Worsted, #4)
    Lion Brand "Vanna's Choice", Fisherman
    Lion Brand "Vanna's Choice", Scarlet

Taffy Twirl (Worsted, #4)
    Lion Brand "Vanna's Choice", Pink Grapefruit
    Loops & Threads "Impeccable", Sunny Day

Pinwheel Pop (Worsted, #4)
    Lion Brand "Vanna's Choice", Periwinkle
    Lion Brand "Vanna's Choice", Pistachio

Cut-Out Cookies (Worsted, #4)
    Lion Brand "Vanna's Choice", Beige
    Lion Brand "Vanna's Choice", Fisherman
    Lion Brand "Vanna's Choice", Scarlet
    Lion Brand "Vanna's Choice", Lemon

Lion Brand "Vanna's Choice", Honey
Lion Brand "Vanna's Choice", Aquamarine
Lion Brand "Vanna's Choice", Fern
Lion Brand "Vanna's Choice", Pink

ANIMAL FRIENDS

Snowy Owl (Worsted, #4)
Lion Brand "Vanna's Choice", Fisherman
(DK, Light Worsted, #3)
Stylecraft "Special DK", Cream
Stylecraft "Special DK", Black
(Super Fine, #1)
Loops & Threads "Woolike", Black

Mouse (Worsted, #4)
Lion Brand "Heartland", Mount Rainier
Lion Brand "Heartland", Denali
Lion Brand "Heartland", Acadia

Lion (Worsted, #4)
Lion Brand "Heartland", Great Sand Dunes
Lion Brand "Heartland", Black Canyon
Lion Brand "Heartland", Acadia

Snowshoe Hare (Worsted, #4)
Lion Brand "Heartland", Acadia
Lion Brand "Heartland", Denali
Lion Brand "Heartland", Black Canyon

Fox (Worsted, #4)
Lion Brand "Heartland", Acadia
Lion Brand "Heartland", Yosemite
Lion Brand "Heartland", Black Canyon

Camel (Worsted, #4)
Lion Brand "Heartland", Great Sand Dunes
Lion Brand "Heartland", Black Canyon
Lion Brand "Vanna's Choice", Cranberry
Lion Brand "Vanna's Choice", Wisteria
Lion Brand "Vanna's Choice", Fern
Lion Brand "Vanna's Choice", Aquamarine

Polar Bear (Worsted, #4)
Lion Brand "Heartland", Acadia

Cat (Worsted, #4)
Lion Brand "Heartland", Bryce Canyon
Lion Brand "Heartland", Yellowstone
Lion Brand "Vanna's Choice", Denali
Lion Brand "Vanna's Choice", Acadia

Dog (Worsted, #4)
Lion Brand "Heartland", Great Sand Dunes
Lion Brand "Heartland", Black Canyon

Penguin (Worsted, #4)
Lion Brand "Vanna's Choice", Fisherman
Lion Brand "Vanna's Choice", Black
Lion Brand "Vanna's Choice", Terracotta

BABY'S FIRST CHRISTMAS

Baby Girl (Worsted, #4)
Lion Brand "Vanna's Choice", Beige
Lion Brand "Vanna's Choice", Black
Red Heart "Baby Soft Steps", Baby Pink

Baby Boy (Worsted, #4)
Lion Brand "Vanna's Choice", Beige
Lion Brand "Vanna's Choice", Black
Lion Brand "Vanna's Choice", Honey
Lion Brand "Vanna's Choice", Sky Blue
Lion Brand "Vanna's Choice", Colonial Blue

Other Books by Linda Wright

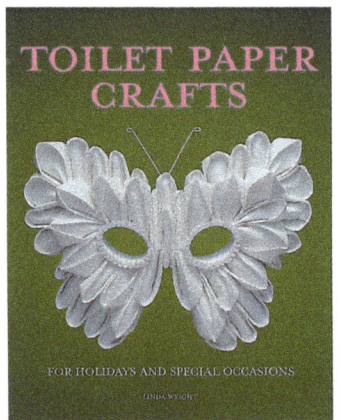

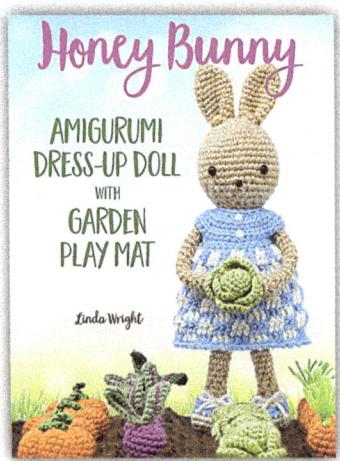

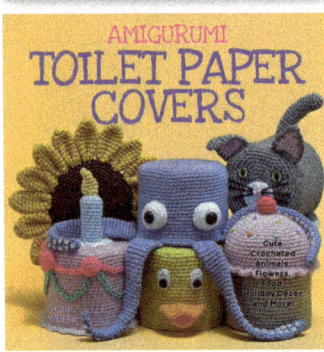
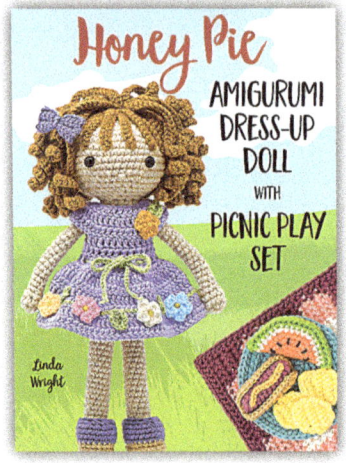
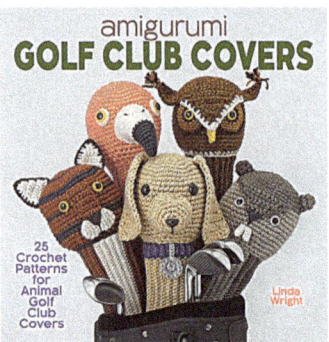
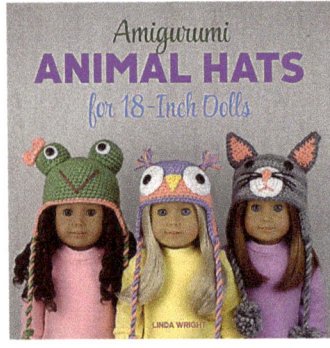

LINDA WRIGHT studied textiles and clothing design at the Pennsylvania State University. She is the author of various handicraft books including the groundbreaking *Toilet Paper Origami*, its companion book, *Toilet Paper Origami On a Roll* and numerous works of amigurumi-style crochet. To learn more about these fun-filled books, visit:

amazon.com/author/lindawright   pinterest.com/LindalooEnt   lindaloo.com

www.ingramcontent.com/pod-product-compliance
Lightning Source LLC
Chambersburg PA
CBHW060939170426
43194CB00027B/3000